The
Inevitable
Choice

EDMUND DAVISON SOPER

THE
INEVITABLE
CHOICE

Vedanta Philosophy or Christian Gospel

ABINGDON PRESS

NEW YORK   NASHVILLE

THE INEVITABLE CHOICE

Copyright © MCMLVII by Abingdon Press

Library of Congress Catalog Card Number: 57-5080

SET UP, PRINTED, AND BOUND BY THE
PARTHENON PRESS, AT NASHVILLE,
TENNESSEE, UNITED STATES OF AMERICA

PREFACE

The fascination of the East is exercising an increasing influence upon men and women in the West. So far has this proceeded that in many cases Westerners have accepted the philosophical outlook and even the religion of Buddhists and Hindus. To a limited extent this is true of the teachings of the Zen sect of Buddhism in Japan. But it is the form of Hinduism in India known as the Vedanta which has been attracting the interest, capturing the imagination, and securing the adherence and loyalty of large numbers of the intelligentsia of Western Europe and America. And even when Vedanta has not been embraced as the one true philosophy of life, it has entered, sometimes almost unconsciously, the minds and influenced the thinking of many who have been thus turned away from their loyalty to their ancestral faith and who are led to doubt the validity of the Christian claim that the revelation of God in Jesus Christ is the one completely adequate message for mankind.

It is to meet this situation that this book is written. The need for such a presentation is the greater because of the unique character of the approach made by the proponents of the Vedanta. Christianity has always met opposition. It is the atmosphere in which the religion of Christ has thrived whenever it has been true to its genius and active in propagating its message to the ends of the earth. But in the present day in its connection with the Hindu Vedanta it has come into contact with a new kind of attitude and propaganda. Christians are told that it is not

5

necessary for them to separate themselves from their Christian teaching or their church, that the new doctrine which is being presented is not out of harmony with the truth they have known since they were children. Of course they are confronted with a new doctrine which is described as all-comprehensive and which will solve all the problems which have been troubling them and the rest of the world in this time of danger and uncertainty.

Herein lies the danger of this new doctrine. When its all-embracing new teachings are clearly understood, it becomes evident that they dissolve into mere words the essential meaning of the Christian gospel and render the Christian mission in the world a useless task.

In order to present the full meaning of the Vedanta, it has been necessary to see it in its right perspective. This has led to a consideration of a number of aspects of Hinduism out of which the Vedanta has emerged and without which it would be difficult if not impossible to realize its true nature.

This book is not intended for the specialist in Hinduism and the Vedanta philosophy, however. For him there is a large and ever-increasing list of books and pamphlets prepared by both Indian and Western scholars. What I have in mind is the growing number of men and women who are becoming interested in Indian thought and its relevance to the life of the world today but who will never be able to delve into the original sources.

These thoughts have been in my mind for many years. I was born in Japan and have had contact with the East all my life. For over forty years I have been studying and teaching the religions of the world in colleges and theological seminaries. Since my retirement I have lived three years in the East, two years of which were spent in teaching Indian religions to Indian students for the Christian ministry. Upon my return to this country I discovered anew how deeply Eastern religious philosophy, notably that of the Vedanta, was influencing the thought and life of men and women in America and Europe. In many cases I feel sure this change in viewpoint is due to an inadequate understanding of what the Vedanta involves and also of what Christianity has to offer. This book attempts to deepen the understanding in both areas.

I wish to express my deep gratitude to the Board of Missions of the Methodist Church, which has made the publication of this book possible. I must mention especially Dr. James K. Mathews, the executive secretary of the Division of World Missions, who initiated the project with the Board, and Dr. Roland C. Scott, who in Dr. Mathew's absence did most valuable service in suggestions for revision of the manuscript.

It is impossible for me to express adequately my gratitude to Dr. Henry E. Kolbe, professor of Christian ethics in Garrett Biblical Institute, my former student and colleague, who unsparingly and painstakingly has read the entire manuscript twice and has pointed out infelicities and inadequacies in many places.

My thanks are also due to Mrs. Betty Beeman and to Mrs. Betty Halford, who typed these pages and with patience and skill smoothed out a much-mangled manuscript. Nor can I do justice to my wife for encouragement in the entire process of preparing this book and for the care with which she worked with me in the last stages of the preparation of the manuscript for publication.

EDMUND D. SOPER

1202 Maple Ave.
Evanston, Illinois

CONTENTS

Chapter One

The Real Encounter

IN face of the overwhelmingly great tasks still ahead of us, the real encounter of the Gospel with the great world religions has as yet scarcely begun." [1] Such a startling declaration, coming from J. C. Hoekendijk, formerly of the secretariat of the World Council of Churches and now professor in the University of Utrecht, Holland, brings us to a halt. Has not Christianity been in contact with the non-Christian religions long enough to have felt the full brunt of their resistance and opposition? From the very beginning, when the new faith began to feel that it was in conflict with Judaism and when a little later it was in the midst of strife with the mystery religions in the Roman Empire, the leaders of the Christian movement have been compelled to evaluate other religions and lead their followers to fit themselves to meet the inevitable rivalry. And this has been true through the centuries, especially during the past 150 years of the modern missionary era. Since the turn of the century—and even before— some of the most monumental and authoritative studies of the religions of the world have come from scholarly missionaries and missionary writers. But a significant change has come over the situation, a change in certain features of the world religions which now present a front quite different from that of a generation ago.

When such a widely read magazine as *Life* publishes six able and splendidly illustrated articles on "The World's Great Re-

[1] *The International Review of Missions*, Vol. XLI, No. 163, July, 1952, p. 330.

ligions," as it did in 1955, we are convinced that there is a popular demand for information on the religions as well as on other features of the life of the nations with which we in the Western world are now being brought into ever closer contact. The first of these articles is on Hinduism. Anyone who reads and studies this article will have a very good, though short, picture of popular Hinduism and of the philosophical movement which now dominates the thinking of the Indian intelligentsia. In the last section of the article, that on "Change and Challenge," a Christian reader will be introduced to certain aspects of modern Hindu thought which, to say the least, will be disturbing. When he reads, for example, that "Hindus themselves think their religion is not only the most ancient in the world but also the most modern and the best suited to resolve the problem of the world's many conflicting faiths," he realizes that a challenge is being thrown down to Christianity, whose followers, almost to a man, have simply taken it for granted that their religion is the only hope of a world torn by animosity and discord. And when he reads further, he is likely to be shocked by such a statement as this: "[The Hindu] considers himself to be the representative of 20th Century understanding, and the Christian, along with the Moslem, to be the epitome of the religious exclusiveness and bigotry which must disappear in the modern world."

One other statement in this article from *Life* brings the issue even closer home to the Christian mind and heart. It is a quotation from an article in the religious weekly *The Christian Century* in which Philip Ashby of Princeton University wrote: "A respected and eminent Indian Christian . . . recently said to me that he is convinced the Hindu . . . argument that all religions are equally valid may well sweep the world in the next twenty-five years. He found this thesis congenial to the contemporary European and American mind." Are all the religions of the world equally valid? This is the question which more than any other lies back of the writing of this book. To put it succinctly and at once, it is my conviction that Christianity is unique, that it has a message which no other religion proclaims, and that there lies before every person in the world the necessity of making a choice between the claims of Jesus Christ and those of the other religions of the world.

This choice is as necessary between Christianity and Hinduism as between Christianity and the other non-Christian religions. The other religions stand in contrast and even opposition to Christianity; but Hinduism in its more recent form, that of the Vedanta philosophy as taught by the Ramakrishna Mission, is the most subtle and powerful and therefore the most dangerous opponent of Christianity in the world today. It is illuminating that an article in a popular magazine should present the facts and pose the question which above all others the Christian world must face in the present day. It would seem that the "real encounter of the Gospel with the great world religions," as Hoekendijk puts it, is really before Christianity and that it is high time that Christians recognize the situation and are preparing themselves to meet it.

Other statements of the same position which has just been presented are being made by Arnold J. Toynbee, the eminent English historian. In an address (November 3, 1955) at Union Theological Seminary in New York he said, "I suggest that we recognize all higher religions as revelations of what is good and right. . . . All the essentials in Christianity have non-Christian precedents and non-Christian parallels in other higher religions," and also that Christians ought "to meet their brothers—the followers of other religions—on the common ground that exists between them and us." [2] The discussion of the validity of such statements as these will occupy us in succeeding chapters, but these references are made here to make clear that there is an "encounter" between Christianity and other faiths different from the relations of our religion with others in the past.

The significance of the stand now being taken by Arnold Toynbee lies in the fact that it is a relatively new attitude on his part. Six volumes of his massive work *A Study of History* were published between 1934 and 1939. The last four volumes did not appear until 1954. In this fifteen years' interval Toynbee shifted his position and greatly surprised his readers and admirers by asserting, among many other statements, that the "writer of the Study will venture to express his personal belief that the four higher religions that were alive in the age in which he was living were four variations on a single theme." [3] Also, and very vigorously, we find him declaring, "In denying that other religions may be *God's chosen and sufficient channels* for revealing Himself to some human souls, it seems to me to be guilty of blasphemy. If it is inadmissible to call oneself a Christian without holding these tenets, then I am not entitled to call myself a Christian." [4] So we begin to discover that leaders of thought in the Western world are thinking the same thoughts with Hindu proponents of the Vedanta philosophy. But it is only one item; many more instances of the prevalence of such thinking will be forthcoming as we proceed. We may also begin to realize what a change in the typical Christian attitude would be necessary were we to come over to the position which Arnold Toynbee now occupies.

[2] *Information Service* of the Bureau of Research and Survey of the National Council of Churches, Vol. XXXIV, No. 41, December 10, 1955.
[3] *A Study of History*, VII, 428.
[4] *Ibid.*, n. 2 (the italics are mine).

New movements are being organized and new interpretations offered which present these faiths in a different light. They make possible the adherence of enlightened and educated men to ancient religions which in their traditional garb had in varying degrees lost their hold. Those who have come into contact with Western thought with its scientific outlook and historical criticism find it difficult if not impossible to accept the old myths and legends and to give themselves to the incongruous practices of the various cults. As a result new schools of thought have arisen which seek to win the confidence of men who are emancipated from at least certain features in their traditional outlook. The leaders in these movements not only are versed in the lore of their own religious past but have given themselves to a study— more or less profound—of what the West has to offer. This is particularly true of Christianity, which they find around them almost everywhere engaged in an aggressive campaign to win the allegiance of men and women to Jesus Christ. A sizable number of these intelligentsia have come into the Christian Church, but the vast majority hold aloof. They continue to believe strongly that their own faith is sufficient to meet their needs if reinterpreted in the light of modern thought.

This stage has not been reached in all the religions, notably in the primitive religions of the backward animistic peoples scattered over the earth. As soon as these people begin to be enlightened, their old animistic ideas fail to function and they readily become converts to other faiths such as Buddhism, Islam, and Christianity. This has taken place for many centuries and is still going on. Buddhism became the recognized religion in Ceylon, Burma, and Thailand in an early day, taking the place of the animistic faith which had prevailed from time immemorial. For several centuries Islam has been moving southward into central Africa and is today superseding the traditional faith of Negroes and

Bantus with comparatively little opposition. Centuries ago this faith penetrated the Malay world and replaced its animistic faith—and also the weakened and degenerate forms of Buddhism and Hinduism—in Malaya, Sumatra, Java, and other islands of Indonesia. We of Europe and North America must remember that the simple faith of our Celtic, Teutonic, and Slavic ancestors was a primitive animism and that it offered little opposition to the monks who were responsible for the conversion of northern Europe to Christianity. In many lands even down to the present day the same transfer is taking place from animistic paganism to the Christian faith.

The situation is very different in the case of Islam. The new religion developed in opposition to Christianity, from which it appropriated some features while violently rejecting others. Islam soon began to construct a theology based on the principles of the Greek Aristotle. This theology remains today the standard of orthodoxy. It is thoroughly medieval, its processes being those of the Schoolmen of the Middle Ages. We of the West have left behind that viewpoint under the influence of the new scientific views of the universe and the principles of historical criticism. There can be little encounter on high levels between Islamic and Christian thought so long as this attitude remains dominant in Islam.

There are evidences, however, of a different outlook on the part of a number of leaders in Islamic thought, notably in India. There are the founding of the Muslim University at Aligarh, built on modern lines, by Syed Ahmad Khan, and the appearance of such volumes as The Spirit of Islam, by Ameer Ali, and The Reconstruction of Religious Thought in Islam, by Sir Muhammed Iqbal. Even more recently (1952) two chapters in Moral Principles of Action: Man's Ethical Imperative, a volume containing chapters by leading authorities on ethics East

16

and West, were contributed by Muslims. Sir Muhammed Zafrullah Khan writes on "Moral Principles as the Basis of Islamic Culture" and Khalifa Abdul Kakim on "One God, one World, One Humanity." It is exceedingly interesting to note that both these writers are connected officially with the new Islamic state of Pakistan and write to commend their views to the world into which they have so recently emerged.

And yet none of these leading thinkers in Islam, or any others in the Islamic ranks, have felt called upon to bring their thinking into line with Western procedure at two vital points: They have not allowed the light of modern criticism to question the absolutist claims made for the Koran as the actual uncreated word of Allah, or to bring the principles of historical criticism to bear on the life and character of Mohammed the Prophet. He still remains the unchallenged example of the ideal man, the paragon of excellence at every point in his life and his dealings with others. It is difficult, if not impossible, to feel that there is even yet a real point of contact between the two religions except that of rather violent opposition and conflict, mitigated in many cases by the friendliness which exists between individual Muslims and Christians.

We find ourselves in another world when we come into the realm of Buddhism and Hinduism. A distinction must at once be made between the popular forms in which both these religions are practiced and the newer movements which are reinterpreting these faiths and are offering a very different front to thinking men both East and West. Popular Buddhism and Hinduism need not be taken very seriously from the standpoint of any appeal they might make to the intellect of modern man. If the practices are not puerile and even revolting, as they are in places, there is still nothing about them that could be looked upon as challenging the thinking of men looking for a valid and

17

reasonable faith. S. Radhakrishnan says of Hinduism what an outsider would hesitate to put down in black and white. Here are his words: "Hinduism . . . is admirable and abhorrent, saintly and savage, beautifully wise and dangerously silly, generous beyond measure and mean beyond all example." [5] Many educated men, it is unfortunately true, do go through the forms of worship and keep many of the prescribed regulations; but they do so with little or no belief in their validity. Habit is strong, and the powerful pressure of tradition and family and community custom is often too strong to resist. But this conformity to custom and habit is very different from aggressive effort to justify these beliefs and practices at the bar of the thought life of people today.

When, however, we are introduced to the Buddhism and Hinduism of highly trained and keenly intelligent leaders of these modern movements, the situation presents a very different aspect. This is true in both these great religions, but especially in Hinduism, with which we are particularly concerned in this study. But even though in a lesser way reinterpretations are making headway in Buddhism, these movements are highly significant. We shall have occasion to call attention at several points in the following discussion to these Buddhist movements, especially where, as in the Zen sect in Japan, interpretations quite similar to those in the newer Hinduism are being promulgated and are finding lodgment in circles widely scattered in the West. These developments in Japanese Buddhism are taking place in the Mahayana, the form of the faith now found in central and eastern Asia. The distinguished scholar, D. T. Suzuki, professor in the Otani University, Kyoto, Japan, is producing a series of volumes on Zen Buddhism which in their English dress are

[5] *Eastern Religions and Western Thought*, p. 338.

exerting a strong influence. They are being published under the auspices of the Buddhist Society of London. Certain Westerners, such as Christmas Humphreys, president of the Buddhist Society, and Dwight Goddard, a former Congregationalist missionary to China from America, have espoused the Zen interpretations and are presenting this form of Buddhism to the West as the most satisfying doctrine of life and the universe.

The Buddhism of Ceylon, Burma, and Thailand is quite different from the Mahayana of the North. It is commonly known as Hinayana though its adherents greatly prefer it to be called Theravada, the "way of the Elders." It is the form of Buddhism which is in much deeper conformity with the teaching of Gautama Buddha himself and that of the earlier leaders of the faith in India. A revival is taking place among the Theravadins. A World Fellowship of Buddhists has been formed, whose president is G. P. Malalasekara, professor in the University of Ceylon. This erudite scholar is welcomed as a lecturer in leading American universities and learned societies.

Another evidence of a revival among the Theravadins was the holding of the Sixth World Buddhist Council, which met in the city of Rangoon, Burma. This council was opened in May, 1954, and continued until May, 1956. The first council was held 2,500 years ago just after the death of the Buddha, and now the sixth council in Rangoon. The Burma parliament in 1951 passed a bill authorizing the holding of a council "for the solution of the problems confronting mankind. . . . to overcome greed, hatred and delusion, which are at the root of all the violence, destruction and conflagration consuming the world." What is the purpose of the Chatta Sangayana, as the sixth council is called? It is to "radiate rays of peace through the whole world"—so runs the official statement. Homer A. Jack also informs us that an "international Buddhist University" is contem-

19

plated and that a new Buddhist library is planned, for which the American Ford Foundation has appropriated $250,000. Is there any wonder that Jack should close his article in the *Christian Century* with such a statement as this: "This renaissance of Buddhism cannot but have an important effect on the whole world"? [6]

It is when we come to Hinduism, however, that the full scope and power of the renewed vitality of an Eastern religion can best be studied. The Vedanta philosophy is an integral factor in historical Hinduism, so it is necessary constantly to keep in mind its backgrounds in the history of the religion. What we are about to consider in this book is not a movement in Hinduism as a whole, and yet it is intimately involved in the story of the religion during the centuries. The encounter of Hinduism with Christianity and Western culture as a whole has been brought into sharp focus through a movement which has taken organized form in the Ramakrishna order of celibate monks. It is this group which has taken up the task of preaching and teaching the Vedanta view of life and destiny through what is known as the Ramakrishna Mission. While this organized order is the aggressive spearhead of the movement, the Vedanta teachings have been accepted so widely that they have become the belief of educated and cultured Hindus very widely indeed. This philosophy is frequently referred to as Neo-Hinduism or Essential Hinduism to distinguish it from the popular religion of the masses. In order the more clearly to appreciate the meaning and scope of this development, we may at the very beginning of this study look at it from three angles.

1. *Hinduism has been passing through a period of revival.* It is a period so significant that it is worthy of the attention and

---

[6] "The Buddhist World Council," July 6, 1955.

serious study of all those who are following the course of religion in the world. We must keep our eyes on India, for that land is par excellence the land of religion in the world. All the religions are there, and nowhere else can the study of religions be pursued with greater advantage. When Hinduism, which has the largest number of adherents in that country, is in the midst of a vigorous revival, it behooves us to look into it with care.

The revival had its beginning after a long period of decline. Hindus themselves realize this and have acknowledged it frankly. Speaking of India after the Great Mutiny of 1857 and the taking-over of the government from the East India Company by the British Crown and Parliament in 1858, D. S. Sarma declares:

> Her own civilization and culture had been at the lowest ebb for over a hundred years from about the middle of the eighteenth century. In that dark period nothing of first-rate importance was produced in any language, there was no new development in Hinduism and almost all indigenous arts languished and died owing to lack of patronage and even of appreciation.[7]

He quotes from an Indian newspaper, the *Amrita Bazaar Patrika*, which declared in 1879: "What can the doctor do when the patient is already stiff and cold? India is dead to all sense of honour and glory. . . . Talk of regenerating India to the Indians! You might as well talk to the sands of the sea."[8]

But a revival came. How can it be accounted for? There is complete agreement on the part of both Indian and Western scholars at this point. The British government and Christian missionaries introduced India to Western education and learning. This was facilitated by the famous "note" of Lord Macaulay,

[7] *Studies in the Renaissance of Hinduism in the Nineteenth and Twentieth Centuries* (Benares Hindu University, 1944), p. 67.
[8] *Ibid.*, p. 209.

then (1833) Law Member of the Governor-General's Council in India and later the famous historian of England, which decreed that English was the language in which education in India should be conducted. This laid open to the rising generation the riches of English literature, filled with thoughts entirely new to the Indian mind. The influence of such education has been profound. Besides this new kind of appeal to the Indian intellect and conscience there is to be added the philanthropic work which began to spread and to be deeply appreciated by a people in very sore distress. Hospitals and clinics, hygiene and sanitation, doctors and nurses, famine relief and orphan homes, and other charitable services began their work. Again it was the British rulers and the missionaries who initiated these forms of helpfulness, later to be taken up and carried on by the Indians themselves.

To these causes must be added one of a very different kind. During the period of decline in Indian culture their ancient literature was for the most part a closed book, until—and here a surprising thing took place—it was rediscovered not by Indian but by European scholars. All were amazed at the wealth of beauty and wisdom hidden away in these ancient texts, now brought to light in new annotated editions and translations. This reclaimed literature came as a new revelation to the Indians themselves, who seized upon it and made it the basis of what to them was a well-nigh new interpretation of life and religion. For many years now the leaders in Indian religions and philosophical thought have been claiming that what they are teaching is the wisdom of the Rishis, saintly men who in the long ago received these revelations directly from the deities who were worshiped by the Indians in the days of the pristine glory and purity of their faith.

All these influences toward reinterpretation were at work

during the latter decades of the nineteenth century, but they were intensified and accelerated by the movement toward independence. Here the name of Mohandas K. Gandhi stands out without a peer. Undoubtedly he was one of the greatest men of modern times. He is fittingly called the Father of Indian Independence. Had it not been for him, it is hard to tell when India would have secured her freedom. This little man would not listen to the use of military power but placed his dependence on "soul force" (*Satyagraha*). Others, notably Nehru, also played an important role. World War II undoubtedly brought matters to a climax so that independence was achieved at its close almost unexpectedly. On August 15, 1947, the British army and civil servants sailed away, never to return. India was free, and her own administrators took over the reins of government of a new and independent country among the nations of the world. That event marks an era in world history; the age of colonialism was passing away. All Asia is feeling the repercussions, and the end is not yet.

We are interested here in the effect of this revolution on the cultural and religious life of India. The change came as an electric shock; joy filled the air as the people felt released from the frustrations of foreign rule. All the movements toward the revival of things Indian received a tremendous impetus. "India for the Indians" became a watchword. Foreign influences were depreciated, and everything Indian was exalted. Their culture and religion were declared superior to anything else in all history in any part of the world! Listen to the enthusiastic rhapsody of Sarma:

There is no doubt that Hinduism today is as fresh and vigorous as it was in any of the periods we have considered. . . . We have no longer any fear that it might be overpowered by Christianity or Western civilization. It has outlived the Christian propaganda of modern times as it outlived the Muslem oppression of the middle ages and the Buddhist schism of ancient days. It is now able to meet any of these world religions on equal terms as their friend and ally in a common cause.[9]

"As their friend and ally in a common cause"—that is a new note of high significance in the present situation. There is resistance to the advance of Christianity, which at times reaches the point of outright persecution. But among most of the advanced leaders Christianity, with its estimated nine million adherents, is accepted as a permanent feature in the religious scene. One of the conclusions arrived at by these students is that all religions are equally true and that it makes little or no difference to what faith a man gives his allegiance—are they not striving for the common welfare, and will they not all reach the same goal? It is this feature, in addition to others, which makes Hinduism in its recent developments so fascinating and important for us of the West to understand and appreciate.

2. *Hinduism presents the possibility of a syncretism of Hinduism and Christianity.* This can be said of no other religion in its relations with our faith. What would take place if this were to happen would be the disappearance of Christianity as a separate, distinct religion. It has even been said that the Christian Church might become just one of the sects which make up what is known as Hinduism, but with its gospel sadly altered or completely destroyed.

This danger can be appreciated by a study of one of the most important events in the history of Indian religion. It will be recalled that Sarma in the quotation above stated that Hinduism had "outlived . . . the Buddhist schism of ancient days." From the standpoint of the relations of one religion with another

* *Ibid.,* pp. 69-70.

that is just about the most illuminating episode in the entire history of the world's religions. The story is important but can be referred to here only in briefest outline. The dates of Gautama the Buddha, the founder of Buddhism, are approximately 563 to 483 B.C. He was a Hindu and never formally left his ancestral faith. He could not agree with certain doctrines which were being propounded by Hindu leaders and arrived at conclusions seriously at variance with his early training in Hinduism. But he never broke with the faith and seemed to think of what he was teaching as a reform movement in the old religion. But by gathering a group of devoted followers around him and organizing a monastic order he made inevitable the severing of ties between his followers and those in the Hindu community. It soon became evident that a new religion had been born.

For a thousand years Buddhism thrived as a rival system. In fact in 273 B.C. the Buddhist Emperor Asoka ascended the throne and ruled almost the entire country for forty years. He was without doubt the most enlightened ruler India ever had. He was not only a follower of the Buddha by profession, but he ruled his enormous realm according to the principles which he professed. Inscriptions and edicts on pillars and rocks scattered over the country attest to this day his earnest devotion to the religion he had accepted. Indians produced no histories in the ancient days, so the story is vague at many points. We do know, however, that Buddhism was still strong at the beginning of the fifth century A.D. After two hundred years its decline was very evident, as is attested by Chinese pilgrims who came to study Buddhism in the land of its birth. By the eleventh century, when the Muslims invaded the country, it was so weak that only a few groups were able to hold themselves together as a separate people. There is no Buddhism in India proper today except little colonies at several sacred shrines where, largely through outside influence, centers have been established to which pilgrims come from foreign countries. There is Buddhism in nearby Nepal, Burma, Thailand, and Ceylon, and also, farther off, in Tibet, Mongolia, China, Korea, and Japan; but in India there is none.

The reason for repeating these facts here is to provide background for the question, How account for the complete disappearance of a great and powerful religion from a country which had given it birth and in which for so long it exercised a powerful influence? The answer to that question may shed light on the danger which many believe is real in the case of Christianity in India at the present time.

There are two sides to the answer to this question: In the first place, the disappearance of Buddhism cannot be accounted for by asserting that it was mainly the result of persecution. There are writers who claim that there was no persecution at all, and others take the opposite view. The subject is a difficult one owing to the want of sufficient direct evidence. But on the other hand, it is easy to prove that there was vigorous, very vigorous, opposition on the part of Hindu leaders in the tenth and eleventh centuries A.D. This opposition was of a literary kind; how effective it was will probably never be known.

Setting these efforts of its opponents aside as of secondary importance, emphasis must be laid, in the second place, on the marvelous power of absorption which has always been possessed by Hinduism. It seems able to take into itself and assimilate almost any doctrine or movement with which it comes into contact. This is what took place in the case of Buddhism. Not that Buddhism did not affect Hinduism and cause real changes. One of these is the remarkable fact that before the coming of Buddhism the slaughter of animals in the sacrificial system was the rule in Hinduism. That has almost completely ceased; only

26

in a few places can bloody sacrifices be found in present-day India. The Buddhist doctrine of ahimsa, or nonviolence, prevailed and became a guiding principle in the ritual of sacrifice in Hinduism. But—and this is the important fact—what ultimately issued from the contact of the two faiths was not an amalgam; rather it was Hinduism with its historical continuity unimpaired, with very little of Buddhism in the final outcome.

The explanation of this strange and remarkable blotting out of a once powerful religion has still another side. Buddhism came up out of Hinduism; and while it became separate and distinct and repudiated much that Hinduism stood for, it still had a strong family likeness and so was the more readily reabsorbed by its parent faith. There seems not to have been sufficient difference to keep it from being so toned down that it was swallowed and digested with comparatively little difficulty. Hinduism was and remains a social system, family and caste being organic to its very life. On the other hand Buddhism did not materially affect the organization of Hindu society. It was at its core a monastic system, men and women being separated from the social organization of the people and living a life apart. When Islam swept into India, Hinduism because of its social solidarity was able to withstand the attack, while Buddhism could not resist the onslaught and disappeared.

But how can we account for the fact that except in the case of the disappearance of animal sacrifice so little of what was distinctive in Buddhism was carried over into Hinduism? Again there is no direct evidence, but it would seem that by slow attrition Buddhism was reduced more and more into likeness to Hinduism until there was little left to carry over. As already said, Hinduism seems able to masticate and digest almost any doctrine or theory or practice unless it is very sharply in opposition to what is Hindu and unless that unique thing is held very firmly and intelligently by its adherents. To all of which must be added "that Buddhism labored under a helpless inner decay," so that it was a "degenerate and Hinduized Buddhism" which came to its end in India.[10]

There is another illustration of the same tendency at the present time. The religion of the Sikhs is the youngest and one of the lesser religions of India, consisting of something over six million adherents, nearly all of whom are in the north. The founder Nanak (A.D. 1469-1538) started out with the purpose of uniting Hindus and Muslims in one fellowship. He failed in this attempt and set up a religion of his own which has had a striking history. Sikhism soon found that Islam was its enemy. Two of its gurus, or leaders, were assassinated by the Mogul rulers, so that there has been a deadly hatred of Islam, which has continued with unabated bitterness to our day. But friendliness has come more and more to exist between the Sikhs and Hindus, so much so that it is predicted that Sikhism will be drawn back again into the Hindu fold. At a reception given in New Delhi since Independence Day in commemoration of the birth of Nanak, attended by Hindus as well as Sikhs, Rajendra Prasad, president of the republic of India, a strict Hindu, made an important statement. He said that "Guru Nanak had demonstrated that the same fundamental principles underlay all great religions. He taught his followers not to be misled by the apparent differences of religions, but to concern themselves with fundamentals." [11] One of their own political leaders, Tara Singh, in an address before a conference of the All-India Sikh Students Federation was bold enough to advise "Sikhs to unite

[10] C. H. S. Ward, *Buddhism*, II, *Mahayana*, 108, 110.
[11] *The Statesman*, November 25, 1950.

28

with Hindus." He said that "difficult times were facing the country and [he] expected the students to contribute their mite and unite with the Hindus." [12] In one of the latest books (1953) on Sikhism, entitled *The Sikhs*, written by Khushwant Singh, himself a Sikh, we read with amazement the first sentences in the Preface: "The chief reason for my writing an account of my people is the melancholy thought that contemporary with my labors are being written the last chapters of the story of the Sikhs. By the end of the century, the Sikhs themselves will have passed into oblivion." At the end of the volume we find the following: "If the process [of assimilation] continues at the present rate, within a short period of history (fifty years at the most) we may witness the remarkable phenomenon of a religious community which achieved the semblance of nationhood disappear in the quicksands of Hinduism." [13]

An important clue to the understanding of this amazing facility to absorb other faiths lies in the fact that Hinduism is the most amorphous of all religions. It is as difficult to take hold of and confine it in one's grasp as a dense fog. What is Hinduism and who is a Hindu? Govinda Das, a former professor in the Benares Hindu University, declared that Hinduism could not be defined, that "Hinduism is absolutely indefinite," that it is an "anthropological process to which, by a strange irony of fate, the name of 'religion' has been given. . . . It is all-comprehensive, all-absorbing, all-tolerant, all-complacent, all-compliant." [14] In Hinduism a man may believe what he likes, do as he pleases, and follow any ritual or custom he chooses and still be a Hindu. A Hindu is a person "who does not repudiate that designation," or one "who says he is a Hindu, and

[12] *Ibid.*, October 12, 1949.
[13] P. 180.
[14] *Hinduism*, p. 45.

accepts any of the many beliefs, and follows any of the many practices that are anywhere regarded as Hindu." [15]

3. *Hinduism has recently begun to influence the thinking of the West.* It has traditionally been a religion for India only with no thought of any propaganda in foreign countries. But in a remarkable fashion in very recent years the West, particularly England and the United States, has felt the impact upon its thought life of Hinduism and the Vedanta philosophy. Over a hundred years ago the religious reformer Ram Mohan Roy, founder of the theistic church, the Brahmo Samaj, visited England and was most hospitably received. This is not difficult to understand since the church which he established was based on belief in one God, the God he had come to accept after careful study of the Islamic Koran and the scriptures of the Old and New Testaments. Unable to accept the unique divinity of Christ, Ram Mohan Roy was virtually a Unitarian; and in our day the Brahmo Samaj is recognized as in fellowship with the Unitarians of the United States. [16]

It was not, however, until much later that the West really became conscious of the meaning of the newer aspects of Hinduism. Only when Swami Vivekananda was introduced to the World Parliament of Religions in Chicago in 1893 and electrified the great audience did the star of Eastern religion begin to rise in the Western sky. He was easily the most striking figure at the World Parliament. Coming to the platform he riveted the attention of his hearers as he uttered these words, "It fills my heart with joy unspeakable to rise in response to the warm and cordial welcome which you have given us. I thank you in the name of the most ancient order of monks in

[15] *Ibid.*, p. 57.
[16] Stephen H. Fritchman, ed., *Together We Advance* (1946). Ch. x on Unitarianism in Asia.

the world; I thank you in the name of the mother of religions; and I thank you in the name of the millions and millions of Hindu people of all classes and sects." [17] After the Parliament had closed, Swami Vivekananda toured this country and also England and was received with high acclaim. The news of this widespread and hearty reception in the West preceded him to India so that on his return his journey from one place to another became a triumphal progress—India was now known and had been lifted high in the estimation of the West.

Since that day the contacts of Indian religion and philosophy with Western thought and religion have become frequent and intimate. This is surely as it should be. When East and West in every other phase of their life are beginning to realize that, whether they desire it or not, they must learn to live together in harmony and peace, it is not only natural but of the utmost importance that they begin to think together of the deepest problems which all men face as human beings sharing a common humanity. Underlying the political, economic, social, and educational interchanges which are taking place are views of life, fundamental philosophies, and religious theories which determine their thinking in every other sphere of activity and experience.

Much good can come from the visits of religious thinkers and philosophers back and forth between the opposite sides of the earth. Exchange lectureships are to be welcomed, and they are fortunately increasing in number. An East-West Philosopher's Conference was held at the University of Hawaii during the summer of 1939 and still another in 1949. The results of the conferences have been published, edited by Charles A. Moore, chairman of the department of philosophy at the University of

[17] Quoted in Sarma, op. cit., p. 270.

Hawaii, both of which volumes form a notable contribution to the literature of understanding between East and West.[18] In these volumes scholars from India, China, and Japan as well as the United States seek to make clear the basic thought of their own lands.

Another outstanding contribution is *The Philosophy of Sarvepalli Radhakrishnan* in the Library of Living Philosophers, edited by Paul Arthur Schilpp, professor of philosophy in Northwestern University. This ample volume presents the views of this most eminent Indian thinker together with criticisms of these views, mostly favorable, by twenty or more scholars representing both East and West. One cannot overestimate the importance of the contribution of Radhakrishnan. In a remarkable series of volumes which come flowing from his pen he is making Indian thought known in all the English-speaking world. We cannot but stand in admiration at this scholar, who has been Spalding professor of Eastern religion and ethics in Oxford University, who also in the realm of practical statesmanship was the first ambassador to Moscow and is now vice-president of India.

These contacts are made both by organized movements and as individual enterprises. The Western world has been brought into relation with the East through representatives of Hinduism more directly than through university professors and philosophers. Great Britain and the United States, especially our own land, have become the objects of missionary endeavor and propaganda which is new in the experience of the West. Various Indian swamis, either independent or organized, have taken up residence in or near our large cities. There they meet with individuals and conduct meetings with groups, composed partly

[18] *Philosophy—East and West* (1946); *Essays in East-West Philosophy* (1951).

of the curious-minded but also of earnest seekers after the truth. This is true especially of southern California, which has become noted as the haven of every group of men and women who have some new idea to nourish and propagate. While there are charlatans and quacks in the number, there are also earnest devotees with a sincere desire to lift men and women to a higher level and give them peace and confidence.

Mention may be made of one of these visiting advocates of Indian thought, Paramhansa Yogananda, author of the *Autobiography of a Yogi*. It is "Dedicated to the Memory of Luther Burbank, an American Saint." This volume has been translated into Bengali, Dutch, French, German, Italian, Spanish, and Swedish. It may be secured from the Self-Realization Fellowship in Los Angeles. On the title page of this five-hundred-page volume is a quotation from John 4:48, "Except ye see signs and wonders, ye will not believe." This gives a clue to the contents of this amazing book, which abounds in accounts of astounding miracles related as actual events in our world today. A hundred times over the miracles of the New Testament Gospels are cited as a kind of justification and validation of the marvels performed by these present-day Hindu holy men. Some of the miracles even go beyond those of Jesus as wonder-provoking marvels. When it is asserted that a man appears in person at the same moment to two other persons at long distances from each other, the limits of credulity are about in sight—and this is but a sample. We are reminded a number of times that this holy man or that was a "Christlike character." The likenesses between Hindu teachings and those of Christianity are frequently pointed out with ample quotations from the Old or New Testaments, but unfortunately the interpretation of these passages would not always stand the test of scholarly exegesis.

The use of the term "God" often cannot but be misleading

to a Christian who thinks of God as the personal creator God of the Bible. The idea in the mind of Yogananda is usually that of the impersonal Absolute, Brahman, who is utterly different from the God and Father of our Lord Jesus Christ. To quote, "Theologians have misinterpreted Christ's words"; we are told that

in such passages as "I am the way, the truth, and the life: no man cometh unto the Father, but by me" (John 14:6), Jesus meant, never that he was the sole Son of God, but that no man can attain the unqualified Absolute, the transcendent Father *beyond* creation, until he has first manifested the "son" or activating Christ consciousness *within* creation. Jesus, who had achieved entire oneness with that Christ-consciousness, identified himself with it inasmuch as his own ego had long since been dissolved.[19]

Many other references are of this type. This Self-Realization Fellowship has houses of worship in Los Angeles and in Hollywood and a retreat in a beautiful site on the shore of the Pacific Ocean.

Again, there are others, free-lance Yogis, who find ears attentive to their representations among the sophisticated Hollywood movie actors and actresses and others who belong to that group. As an illustration the *Chicago Daily News* published a series of three full-length, illustrated articles, September 18, 19, 20, 1952, written by Omar Garrison, who knows something about India and the ways of these Yogis. In large headlines on the front pages we find these stacatto statements, "The Heiress and the Mystic—$100 Million Fails—Doris Duke Finds Her Place in Yoga—Rich Girl Sits at Hindu's Feet to Absorb Secrets of the Orient." Speaking of the reality of Doris Duke's experience, the reporter says, "I know, because I have watched

[19] 3rd ed., p. 179.

serenity erase the tense lines of her face as she sat cross-legged on the floor with him, and chanted the ancient Sanskrit hymn of peace, the 'Gayatri': 'Om bhuhu! . . . Om bhuvaha! . . . Om Sivaha.'" But, strangely enough, at the end of the third article we read, "Has the Yogi really brought permanent peace of mind, and a new happiness to Doris Duke, then? The answer may be yes. It may be no. For Rao [the Yogi], and the yoga he teaches, are like India itself—a mysterious, complex contradiction." Here was a young woman, the daughter of J. B. Duke, the multimillionaire benefactor of Duke University, a girl whose wealth and luxury and two marital experiences had not brought her peace, going to a wandering Yogi to find what her Methodist background had failed to provide. One hesitates to present the two illustrations just given. They are on a very different level from the Hindu mission in the West which is our chief concern in these studies. But these instances demonstrate the fascination which lays hold on people who are hypnotized by the Yogi wonder-worker who in the name of Oriental mysticism weaves his spell of enchantment over the minds of many Western men and women.

Turning away from such illustrations, we are surely ready to consider a much more serious appeal to thoughtful men and women. We will recall the reference to Swami Vivekananda, whose meteorlike appearance before the World Parliament of Religions in 1893 was like an apparition from an unknown world. It was he who founded the Ramakrishna Mission and filled its early representatives with purpose and enthusiasm in their undertakings. But in order to understand Swami Vivekananda we must go back a step to his master and teacher, Ramakrishna Paramahamsa. This remarkable man died in 1886. He was born of a poor but respectable Brahmin family in Bengal and early became a priest of a small Hindu temple a few miles north of Calcutta. But the work which made his life significant was with a group of disciples who gathered around him, the chief of whom was Vivekananda. Sri [Lord or Master] Ramakrishna, as he came to be called, was first of all an ascetic and devotee. He came to the point where both the desire for money and sexual craving seemed to die within him. The wife to whom he was married very early in life was never a wife to him but remained a most devoted attendant and helper and worshiped him as a god. He in turn did reverence to her as the embodiment of the deity to whom he turned on all occasions, the Mother Goddess Kali, whose chief temple is located in Calcutta.

Sri Ramakrishna passed through a series of remarkable experiences which led him to believe that all religions are essentially alike. As a result he set up a number of shrines dedicated to the deities of the religions, Christianity among them, and worshiped before each in turn with no sense of incongruity. This gives the clue to one of the most important tenets of the Ramakrishna Mission, the universality of religion, or the essential unity of all religions. As a result of Swami Vivekananda's organizing ability the Ramakrishna Mission came into being. It exercises a remarkable influence in India and has become the spearhead of the movement of Hinduism into the West. It is an organization of celibate monks bound together by a sense of mission not only to India but to the world. It does its work through many centers in India in which educational and medical work is conducted. The Mission also does a considerable publishing business, which gives their work a more persuasive and far-reaching influence.

The monks are highly educated, intelligent men who in the West, as well as in India, commend themselves to the intelligentsia wherever they are sent. These swamis are to be found in France, Great Britain, and the United States. As many as twelve centers are located in the cities of America alone. A number of these men through their writings and their personal contacts have won an enviable place for themselves in the estimation of Christian leaders. Mention may be made of Swami Akhilananda of Boston. Books from his pen show him to be a man of deep earnestness and appreciation of the needs of human life and of the place of religion in meeting these needs. The introduction of one of these volumes is written by Walter G. Muelder of the Boston University School of Theology, and the foreword to another by the late Edgar S. Brightman, professor of philosophy in Boston University.[20] The introduction to this volume was written by Gordon W. Allport, professor of psychology in Harvard University. And now Swami Nikhilananda, the representative of the Mission in New York, is publishing an edition in four volumes of the principal *Upanishads,* two of which are already available.[21] On the title page of both volumes we find this explanation: "Translated from the Sanskrit with an Introduction embodying a study of Hindu Ethics, and with Notes and Explanations based on the Commentary of Sri Sankaracharya, the great Eighth-century Philosopher and Saint of India." We shall see that the *Upanishads* are one of the three foundation stones on which all the philosophies of Hinduism are based. Many editions and translations of these scriptures are available, but it is likely that this extensive and painstaking work will have a large place among scholars in this country. It will surely have become evident that in the

[20] Books by Swami Akhilananda are as follows: *Hindu View of Christ* (1949); *Hindu Psychology, Its Meaning for the West* (1946); *Mental Health and Hindu Psychology* (1951).
[21] The *Upanishads* (Vol. I, 1949; Vol. II, 1952).

Ramakrishna Mission we have a movement on a high level, one which cannot but be influential in our country.

What has been the effect of this form of Eastern thought on the West? Many subtle influences are apparent. Speeches, articles, and books are being published which can scarcely be quoted as directly dependent on the East and yet give evidence of an atmosphere which directly or indirectly emanates from contact with the Vedanta. There is much in certain forms of Western idealistic philosophy which has the ring of the Vedanta. A Christian Scientist feels quite at home among these philosophers, who can readily agree in the nonexistence of pain, sin, and death as true realities. But aside from this kind of more or less indefinite influence, the number of Western men and women who are avowed followers of the Vedanta is a somewhat startling revelation to those who have not been acquainted with the movement.

Two significant volumes have come from the press, both of which are edited and introduced by Christopher Isherwood.[22] The many contributors are for the most part Indians, swamis of the Ramakrishna order; but there is a plentiful sprinkling of men from the West. Christopher Isherwood himself contributes articles in addition to an extensive introduction in the earlier volume in which he gives an exposition of the Vedanta viewpoint. We hear him say, "Brahman is our real, essential nature. . . . 'Then why do I think I'm myself?' 'Because of your ignorance. Christopher Isherwood is only an appearance, a part of the apparent universe. He is a constellation of desires and impulses. . . . He is changing all the time. He has no essential reality.' " [23] As we shall see, this would certainly

[22] Vedanta for the Western World (1945); Vedanta for Modern Man (1951).
[23] Vedanta for the Western World, pp. 2, 4. Used by permission of George Allen & Unwin, Ltd.

indicate a fairly complete acceptance of the basic viewpoint of the Vedanta.

Aldous Huxley is an extensive contributor. The philosophical world remembers well his *Perennial Philosophy*, which had a wide reading after its publication in 1945. The philosophy which is "perennial" is virtually the same as the Vedanta. "If we ignore the counsels of egoism and alter-egoism, and resolutely march towards the divine East, we shall create for ourselves the possibility of receiving the grace of enlightenment." [24] The East is divine and offers us our only hope both religiously and philosophically. Gerald Heard is another in the list of contributors. He gives a devastating condemnation of Christianity in these words, "Tied to an inadequate world-picture, lacking a psychology, fearing experiment, it had to end in the last and worst mistake of brutal intolerance." [25] It comes as somewhat of a surprise to discover that Gerald Heard, whose writings and addresses are received widely by American college students as expositions of Christ's way of life, should truly and underneath all else be an adherent and advocate of a religious philosophy which would undermine the entire Christian attitude and way of life. He says, "That these truths [of Vedanta] are taught here and that the way to practice them is indicated, is of the greatest value. Here is given a system, when in the West we have only had fragments of true gnosis: here is an empirical science, in comparison with those happy insights and uncoordinated hints which are all the guidance our own tradition can now yield." [26] One other of these Western writers may be mentioned, John Van Druten, a Christian Scientist. We hear him saying, "The practice of petitionary

[24] *Ibid.*, p. 276.
[25] *Ibid.*, p. 54.
[26] *Ibid.*, p. 63.

prayer at all, in fact, is as foreign to Christian Science as it is to any of the 'higher religions' of which Aldous Huxley speaks in the article referred to. 'God,' says Mrs. Eddy, 'is not influenced by man.' And again: 'In order to pray aright, we must . . . close the lips and silence the material senses.' " [27] This is far distant from the words of our Master Christ, who declared, "After this manner therefore pray ye" (Matt. 6:9), and then gave us the words we should use, so familiar to us in the Lord's Prayer.

Mention may also be made of two, among others, who are turning their eyes Eastward and are finding satisfactions which Christianity has not furnished. Floyd H. Ross, professor of world religions in the School of Religion, University of Southern California, has written a book on *The Meaning of Life in Hinduism and Buddhism*. When a writer starts out from the Christian tradition and seeks to understand and appreciate the good things to be found in other religions, he is surely working in the spirit of the Golden Rule and in loyalty to the Master of all truth, the one who declared that it was truth which would set men free. But when that writer consistently depreciates the tradition which was his in the beginning and unfailingly exalts Hinduism and Buddhism, he has clearly left his first love and is seeking elsewhere for what he has not been able to discover in Christ and his religion. We hear the author saying, "The decay of Western civilization—more evident in Europe in recent decades—is paralleled by the decay of Christianity as a vital force." [28] E. G. Lee is quoted with approval when he declares, "The reality of God *in our day* lives beyond the concept of Christ; the latter can no longer do the work that millions of religious, seeking men demand of it. It no longer

[27] *Ibid.*, p. 187.
[28] P. 8.

sounds the bell of truth in their minds because historic conditions have partly destroyed its validity." [29] That comes about as near to a denial of essential Christianity according to the New Testament as one could go without actually saying it in so many words.

Another writer is Alan W. Watts, who has approved himself to the world of scholars through his work on the Zen sect in Japan.[30] He wrote this volume while still formally in the Christian ranks, being a clergyman in the Protestant Episcopal Church and in charge of Canterbury House at Northwestern University. In recent years his connection with the church and with Christian faith has ceased and he has become a promoter of a philosophy closely allied to that of Zen Buddhism of Japan and the Vedanta of India. A later volume is entitled *The Supreme Identity* (1950), which allies him with the form of mysticism in which the human individual disappears and becomes or is already one with the Infinite, the Absolute.

With the intimate contact between East and West which is now and promises to continue to be one of the most significant factors in the life of mankind, it is clear that we are entering a new period in the relations of the religions of East and West. The comparative study of religions has entered a new stage. The contrast between Vedanta and our own religion brings to as definite a focus the fundamental difference between religions as can be found anywhere. In the contrast between the God and Father of our Lord Jesus Christ on the one side and Brahman, the attributeless absolute of the Vedanta philosophy on the other, we are brought face to face with an irreconcilable contrast. It is a contrast which cannot be evaded or bridged

[29] *Mass, Man and Religion*, p. 146.
[30] *The Spirit of Zen* (1936); also *Zen* (1948).

41

over and which demands a decision on the part of all who see its significance. It is a decision which penetrates to the deepest recesses of human life and is fraught with the eternal issues of life and death. "The real encounter of the Gospel with the great world religions" has begun.

Chapter Two

Vedanta: Seed and Fruit

W HAT is the origin of the Vedanta? The claim is made
by its exponents that what they proclaim is not new but the
restatement of teachings which have come down from time
immemorial. In that ancient time "Perfect Knowledge" was
revealed by divine beings and was "heard" by the Rishis, who
clothed it in words. The Rishis were saints or patriarchs, human
beings highly exalted and unique in nature, who in their abode
in the mountain heights of the Himalayas received and passed
on to men the sruti, or inspired literature, which remains to
this day the infallible standard of perfect knowledge or truth.
We read in *Sanatana-Dharma* ("Ancient Truth"), *an Advanced
Text-Book of Hindu Religion and Ethics:*[1]

> The Religion based on the Vedas . . . is the oldest of living Re-
> ligions, and stands unrivalled in the depth and splendour of its
> philosophy, while it yields to none in the purity of its ethical teach-
> ings and in the flexibility and varied adaptation of its rites and
> ceremonies. . . . It is thus adapted to every human need, and there
> is nothing which any religion can supply to add to its rounded
> perfection.[2]

Theoretically all Hindus, even the most modern, acknowledge
the authority of the early writings and believe that everything

[1] "The genesis of the Sanatana-Dharma Text-Books is closely linked with the
name of Dr. Annie Besant and her co-workers, Indian and European, who founded
the Central Hindu College at Benares"—p. vii.
[2] *Ibid.*, p. 13.

they now hold and teach is to be found in them at least in essence.

The Vedas, as the oldest of these writings are called, formed the sacred literature of the Aryans who came into India from west-central Asia toward the beginning of the second millennium before Christ. We do not know the exact time of their coming; they may have arrived in small groups years apart as they came with their flocks and herds and spread out in the Pänjab, the "land of the five rivers" in northwest India, and made it their permanent home. In the presence of many uncertainties about these people we are sure that they formed one branch of the Indo-Europeans, who had for millenniums, it may be, fed their cattle and sheep and goats in the vast hinterland on one side or the other of the Caspian Sea, that is, in western Asia or eastern Europe. We also know that they came from the same background as the Slavic, Teutonic, and Celtic peoples to which we of Europe and America belong. But long before our ancestors had begun to emerge from their barbarism, these Aryans developed a remarkable culture both in Persia (Iran-Aryan) and in India.

The Vedas consist of a number of separate parts, but the most important is the Rig-Veda, Rig meaning "praises" and Veda, "knowledge." It consists of more than a thousand hymns, mostly hymns of praise addressed to the gods. One's immediate impression on reading the hymns of the Rig-Veda is that the religion of these people was polytheism pure and simple, and undoubtedly polytheism is there—do they not worship many gods? But as one goes over these hymns time and again, it becomes apparent that we are dealing with something to which we shall be compelled to give another name. There is a tendency toward unity. The gods seem to merge into one another. The god to whom the hymn we happen to be reading is addressed is approached as if he were the sole god of the universe, as if there were no need of other gods. Strange to say, the same impression is produced when one turns the page where another deity is addressed, and so on from one divine being to another. This is not exactly what we mean by polytheism, where usually the gods have different functions and each is besought to grant the favor which is at his disposal. Several names have been given to this strange phenomenon; the best would seem to be that proposed by Max Müller, who called it "kathenotheism," or the worship of one god at a time. This unique phenomenon— and it *is* unique—of the assimilation or merging of the deities of the Aryan pantheon, is exceedingly important in such a study as this. The Vedanta philosophy of present-day Hinduism is a monism, a complete and all-embracing unity. Yet even back at the very start in the earliest authoritative documents of the faith the beginnings of such a tendency began to make their appearance. We must conclude that we are dealing with a wonderful development and with a remarkable people, a people with an innate philosophical bent with which they were endowed by nature and which they have nourished and developed as the centuries have passed.

It is not necessary to review here the entire Vedic literature. There were four Vedas, the *Rig-Veda*, *Sama-Veda*, *Yajur-Veda*, and *Atharva-Veda*. The *Sama* and *Yajur* are for the most part rearrangements of verses from the *Rig*, made for use in the ritual of sacrifice. The *Atharva-Veda* came later and is on a lower level. In addition we have the *Brahmanas*, long treatises on the sacrifices and their conduct.

But to proceed still further, appended to the *Brahmanas* are pieces of writing quite different in type. They are called *Aranyakas*, treatises to be used "in the forest." That is, there were men among these early Aryans who were not satisfied

45

with a religion so largely sacrificial and who therefore left the haunts of men and went off into the forest for quiet and thoughtful meditation. Here again and at an early day we run into the beginnings of a custom which has led Indians all through the ages to become *sanyasins*, or penniless wanderers, a common sight in the India of today. Yet it is not the *Aran-yakas* themselves which are so important for our study, but a series of writings embedded in the *Aranyakas* and sometimes hard to distinguish from them. They are called the *Upanishads* and are highly important in this history of Indian thought, being one of the three foundation documents on which the whole Vedanta structure is built. There are over a hundred of these treatises, but only about a dozen are of sufficient importance for the student of today. We must give them more than passing attention.

The derivation of the word "Upanishad" is significant. *Upa* (near) plus *ni* (down) plus *sad* (to sit), that is, "sitting down near," referring to a little group of pupils or disciples at the feet of a guru, a guide or teacher. But while this derivation is very commonly given, there is another which, as given by Swami Nikhilananda of the Ramakrishna Mission, reads as follows:

The word Upanishad has been derived from the root *sad*, to which are added two prefixes: *upa* and *ni*. The prefix *upa* denotes nearness, and *ni*, totality. The root *sad* means to loosen, to attain, and to annihilate. Thus the etymological meaning of the word is the Knowledge, or Vidyā, which, when received from a competent teacher, *loosens totally* the bondage of the world, or surely enables the pupil to *attain* (i.e., realize) the Self, or *completely destroys* ignorance, which is responsible for the deluding appearance of the Infinite Self as the finite embodied creature.[3]

[3] *Op. cit.*, I, 11. Used by permission of Harper & Bros.

Hindus are thus divided as to which derivation to accept.

The dates of the rise of these compositions are given as "about 600 to 500 B.C., just prior to the Buddhist revival." [4] The *Upanishads* are a very heterogeneous collection of writings, some short, some long, differing from one another in form and content, with no system or order of co-ordination whatsoever. Out of this congeries of writings there emerges a basic thought which becomes dominant as the central theme of the *Upanishads*, namely, that there is but one reality in the universe, the Absolute or All, called Brahman. Over and over again we shall return to Brahman in our study, for not only is the conception central in the *Upanishads* but it is the dominant and determinative thought in the Vedanta philosophy of modern times.

"No longer is worship or sacrifice or good conduct the requisite of religion in this life, or of salvation in the next. Knowledge secures the latter and disapproves of the former." [5] "Knowledge—not 'much learning' but the understanding of metaphysical truth—was the impelling motive of the thinkers of the Upanishads." [6] What a distance has been traversed from the *Rig-Veda!* While there are hints of something more than polytheism and its crass worship in the earlier work, here in the *Upanishads* we find men living in the world of metaphysical speculation where knowledge takes the place of adoration, worship, and sacrifice.

So difficult and opaque is much of the material in the *Upanishads* that it is subject to varied interpretations by different commentators and writers. This difference in conception of what these writings contain is as true today as in the days of the classical interpreters in the past. There are those who admit

[4] R. E. Hume, tr., *The Thirteen Principal Upanishads*, p. 6. Used by permission of Oxford University Press.
[5] *Ibid.*, p. 58. [6] *Ibid.*, p. 58.

that no one consistent viewpoint prevails through all the *Upanishads*. The latest translator and annotator of the text, S. Radhakrishnan holds no such rigid theory. He says, "Though the Upanishads do not work out a logically coherent system of metaphysics, they give us a few fundamental doctrines which stand out as the essential teaching of the early determinative Upanishads." [7] This writer also puts it down that "the Upanishads describe to us the life of the spirit, the same yesterday, to-day and forever. But our apprehensions of the life of spirit, the symbols by which we express it change with time." [8] On the other hand Shankara, the greatest of Indian philosophers, insists upon the complete consistency of the *Upanishads*, and in this he is followed implicitly by the scholars of the Ramakrishna Mission.

While a commentator such as Swami Nikhilananda is willing to admit that there are "various strands of thought" and that "sometimes contradictions appear," he declares that

the orthodox Hindu view is that the Upanishads are consistent, that they describe a single truth. . . . The Vedantic philosophers support this conclusion by certain accepted means of proof.

But the Western critics maintain that the Upanishads present inconsistent views and that conflicting doctrines may be found even in the same Upanishad. Such a conclusion, according to the Hindu philosophers, is the natural result of the inability of the Western Orientalists to find the thread of harmony. . . . According to Sankaracharya, the sole purpose of the Upanishads is to prove the reality of Brahman and the phenomenality or unreality of the universe of names and forms, and to establish the absolute oneness of the embodied soul and Brahman. [9]

Not only Western Orientalists, however, but notable Hindu

[7] *The Principal Upanishads*, p. 25.
[8] *Ibid.*, pp. 24-25.
[9] *Op. cit.*, pp. 13, 14. Used by permission of Harper & Bros.

philosophers have taken issue with Shankara and his school at a number of fundamental points. We shall see how Ramanuja and Madhva did not believe in the "absoluteness oneness of the embodied soul and Brahman," or that this doctrine is the burden of the *Upanishads*. Reference may be made to the thorough work of J. N. Rawson in his volume *The Katha Upanishad*. In his preface he says that the *Katha* is "deservedly the most popular of the Upanishads. As such it has probably seen more editions than any other." He finds himself differing from Shankara profoundly on the fundamental viewpoint of the *Katha*: "This standpoint I now view definitely theistic." But we must always keep in mind that while there are followers of these later philosophers in India at the present time, the scales are weighted heavily in favor of Shankara, and that it is his interpretation which is winning converts in the Western world.

At places the *Upanishads* rise to lofty heights. The most quoted passage is from the *Brihadaranyaka Upanishad* (I. 3.28), which is thus translated by Robert E. Hume:

> From the unreal lead me to the real!
> From darkness lead me to light!
> From death lead me to immortality!

These wistful words give the mood of the *Upanishads*, an eager desire to see things in their true light and to arrive at the real, or reality. But what about the last word in the quotation, "immortality"? Is that the right word? There are those who think it is not but use the word "deathlessness" in place of "immortality." Here are the words of W. D. P. Hill in his exposition of the *Bhagavadgita* in which he refers to this passage from the *Upanishads*: "This prayer perfectly expresses the Hindu conception of life in this world and of liberation . . . the state

49

of release is a state of eternal freedom from birth and death. . . .
The Christian ideal is positive—the fullness of eternal life;
the Hindu ideal is negative—deliverance from repeated birth
and death.[10] So "deathlessness" is to be preferred to "immortality." With all the remarkable insights which they contain,
to sit down and read the *Upanishads* through continuously is
a real task and in many places not uplifting or rewarding. Hume
sums up his long introduction with this general appraisal: "In
a few passages the Upanishads are sublime in their conception
of the Infinite and of God, but more often they are puerile and
grovelling in trivialities and superstitions." [11]

The *Upanishads* form the first layer of the foundation on
which the Vedanta philosophy is built. There are two other
layers, of which we take up the *Vedanta Sutras* first. They are
also called the *Brahma Sutras*, their subject being the great
Absolute Brahman. *Sutras* are brief, exceedingly condensed
statements of truth, "strings of aphorisms of the briefest and
most pregnant description." [12] To give an illustration, here is
one of the shorter *sutras* as found in the original text, "On
account of its dependence, it fits in." But to make sense at all,
something must be added, so it is rendered thus: "On account
of its dependence (on the Lord) it fits in (with our theory)."
So we can understand the suggestion that the *sutras* are "meaning clues, and were intended as memory aids to long discussions
on any topic which the student had gone through with his
teacher or Guru. . . . The desire for brevity was carried to
such extremes that most parts of the Sutra literature are now
unintelligible, and this is particularly true with respect to the
Vedanta-Sutras which has consequently given rise to divergent

[10] *The Bhagavadgita*, p. 54.
[11] *Op. cit.*, p. 70.
[12] J. N. Farquhar, *A Primer of Hinduism*, 2nd ed., p. 65.

systems." [13] And yet with all the difficulties confronting the student, Rawson speaks of them as "perhaps the most central document for Hindu theology." [14] No consensus has been reached as to their date, which is given all the way from the sixth century B.C. to the fourth century A.D. To read the commentary of Shankara, one would conclude that the only doctrine to be found in these enigmatic sentences is the "identity of the individual soul with God in the strictest possible sense, and in accepting a monism so absolute that the material world is regarded as pure illusion, and the personality of God tends to be crushed out." [15] But it seems quite different in the eyes of Ramanuja. He can find a personal God in the *Sutras* and also a real world and real people. On the other hand the long commentary by Swami Viresavarananda, a member of the Ramakrishna order, is most careful to defend the monistic viewpoint of his master Shankara.

The *Bhagavad-Gita*, the "Lord's Song" (commonly called the *Gita*), is the third layer of the foundation on which the modern Hindu thinker, as well as his brethren for the last thousand years, builds his structure. Put into its present form about two hundred years after the time of Christ, it has had its ups and downs in the estimation of Hindus. Just now it is at a peak of approval and admiration, perhaps higher than it has ever reached before. A short treatise about the size of the Gospel of Matthew, the *Gita* has exerted a tremendous influence. It is often called the "Bible of modern Hinduism." Gandhi gave his testimony that it was his chief source of solace and uplift when he found himself in need of help. It is well known that he had high regard for the Sermon on the Mount and declared that he

---

[13] Swami Vireswarananda, *Brahma-Sutras*, pp. 133, iv.
[14] *The Katha Upanishad*, preface.
[15] J. N. Farquhar, *An Outline of the Religious Literature of India*, p. 127.

put its precepts into practice more faithfully than Christians themselves, but with all that, it was the *Gita* to which he turned for the kind of inspiration which he could not find in the Christian Gospels. We find Farquhar, the Christian scholar, giving his tribute: "The Divine song is the loveliest flower in the garden of Sanskrit literature." [16]

This wonderful little writing is found embedded in the *Mahabharata*, the longest epic in any language in the world. The entire poem is an account of the battle which is said to have been fought between Kurus and Pandavas, closely related families contending for the throne in north India in the fourth millennium before Christ. How much genuine history is embodied in the lengthy account, it is very difficult to determine, perhaps very little. A recent ardent Hindu editor and commentator of the *Gita* takes the story just as it stands and accepts it as reliable history from beginning to end.[17] One finds himself in another atmosphere when he takes up the 1948 edition of the *Gita* by Radhakrishnan, in which historical criticism has done its work.[18]

The *Gita* is an episode in the *Mahabharata*, an episode which is said to have taken place when the two armies are drawn up in battle array ready for the command to fight. In the lull we have pictured the royal commander of the Pandavas, Arjuna, sitting in his chariot in conversation with his charioteer. He hesitates to give the fatal order which will plunge not only his own army but that of his cousins, the Kurus, into the midst of dreadful bloodshed and carnage. He asks the advice of his

[16] *Gita and Gospel*, p. 4.
[17] A. S. P. Ayyar, *A Layman's Bhagavadgita*, 2nd ed. Vol. I. Introduction and frequently in the commentary.
[18] *The Bhagavadgita*.

charioteer, and almost the entire remainder of the *Gita* consists of the charioteer's reply. He not only deals with the immediate situation by urging Arjuna to give the fatal command but goes on to give a glowing picture in which the god Krishna is presented as the object of worship and also as the universal reality into which all will be ultimately merged. Now the charioteer, who to Arjuna was just a charioteer when the conversation began, proves to be none other than the Lord Krishna himself in disguise. Gradually his identity is disclosed until he stands out in all the grandeur and majestic glory of the great Lord of the universe.

What does he proclaim as the way of salvation and the ideal to be held before mankind? All the three ways of salvation in Hinduism are presented as valid—the way of works, the way of loving devotion, or faith, and the way of knowledge. It is hard to think that the *Gita* is a unity; but with that remarkable facility of the Hindu mind to reconcile theories which to us of the West seem to be not only different but inconsistent, Hindu scholars find it easy to believe the poem is of one piece, the work of one author. Radhakrishnan says that "in the *Gita* are united currents of philosophical and religious thought diffused along many and devious courses. Many apparently conflicting beliefs are worked into a simple unity to meet the needs of the time, in the true Hindu spirit, that over all of them broods the grace of God." He declares that in the Indian tradition the "apparently incongruous elements were fused together in the mind of the author and that the brilliant synthesis he suggests ... fosters the true life of the spirit." [19] According to Hill: "The sectarian author wished to insist on the absolute supremacy of Krishna Vasudeva, and at the same time to conciliate the ene-

[19] *Ibid.*, p. 15.

mies of his cult. The poem may be called an uncompromising irenicon." [20]

It is not the purpose here to attempt an exposition of the *Gita*, as profitable as it might be; it is, however, incumbent on us to see how this poem has been used as one of the foundations of the Vedanta philosophy. And here we discover violent opposition between two schools of interpreters, one of which holds that the poem is positively misrepresented when it is made the basis of a monistic viewpoint. This is true not only of some Western scholars but of Indians as well. To quote Farquhar, "The thought that remains in the mind after a perusal of this great work is this—The *Gita* is the cry of the Hindu people for an incarnate Savior." [21] Also: "It is the expression of the earliest attempt made in India to rise to a theistic faith and theology." [22] And with this viewpoint we find the great Indian philosopher Ramanuja in agreement. But not so with others. In a translation by Swami Prabhavananda and Christopher Isherwood we find this statement, "Then, again, the Gita is an exposition of Vedanta philosophy based upon a very definite picture of the universe." [23] And Aldous Huxley in the same volume says, "The Bhagavad Gita is perhaps the most systematic scriptural statement of the Perennial Philosophy. To a world at war . . . it stands pointing, clearly and unmistakably to the only road of escape from the self-imposed necessity of self-destruction." [24] The writers of this volume acknowledge that they lean heavily on the great commentary of Shankara, which posits one sole reality in the universe. But is not

[20] *Op. cit.*, p. 16.
[21] *Gita and Gospel*, p. 32.
[22] *An Outline of the Religious Literature of India*, p. 86.
[23] *Bhagavad-Gita, the Song of God*, p. 2.
[24] *Ibid.*, p. 19.

Krishna presented as a deity, a real being to be worshiped, so clearly that this worship can fairly be looked upon as the emphatic factor in the *Gita?* So it would seem to many in both India and the West; but in the minds of convinced monists all this is to be interpreted as secondary, as temporary, as unreal, as a kind of mirage which disappears when the final truth takes possession of a man's consciousness. Aldous Huxley puts it thus, "The Gita is not primarily concerned with Krishna as an individual, but with his aspect as Brahman, the ultimate Reality." [25] Few things are more baffling to the Western mind than this seemingly irresistible bent to allow a viewpoint which one has adopted to determine his interpretation of such a document as the *Gita.* The fact is that in India there has been perpetual warfare between a monistic philosophy and a theistic faith. And what to us is a sad portent, the monistic philosophy has been winning the victory. There is a strand of theistic religion in Hinduism, but it has had a hard struggle and has usually been driven to cover by the monistic philosophy.

It has seemed necessary to take time to give this presentation of the sources of present-day Indian philosophy, but another step is needed. Centuries after these documents had been written and had been put into the form in which we now have them, we come to the age of the classical philosophers, three of them in particular, who built great systems which to this day are accepted as authoritative. No philosophical work of primary importance has been produced since that day of the brilliant flowering of the Indian philosophical genius. We must always keep in mind that it is upon the work of one of these geniuses, Shankara, that the Vedanta philosophy is founded.

Six schools of Hindu philosophy, called darshanas, or "insights," have arisen, six interpretations of the basic conclusions

[25] *Ibid.,* p. 56.

55

reached by thinkers in the days when the *Upanishads* were taking form. Each is said to have had an originator, of whom little is definitely known. While they differ from one another sometimes sharply, they are all an attempt to interpret the ultimate Reality. Again all are in agreement at another most significant point, and at this point we are able to detect the great difference between philosophy as conceived in India and philosophy as we think of it in the West. For us with our Greek heritage, harking back particularly to Plato and Aristotle, the main purpose of philosophy is intellectual satisfaction. We are intent on securing unity in our view of the universe. There is also deep-lying ethical concern. We want the peace of mind which results from discovering a basic harmony or agreement in the midst of the multitude of objects in this universe of ours. Can we find order in the midst of the apparent confusion which is the first impression coming to one who as a beginner looks out and finds a thousand things with no seeming bond of unity holding them together? The philosophical systems which have arisen in the West may be religious or antireligious, but they are not essentially a part of the religious life of any man or group which adopts and advocates them. Of course, they come very close to religious thought, or theology, in that they, like religion, deal with ultimate Reality; but their objective is not the same. Religion, definite theistic religion in particular, has primarily to do with man's personal relation to an ultimate object of worship, to God, while philosophy is concerned with an intellectual problem, seeking a basis for interpreting the universe which is calculated to give cohesion to a person's thinking about himself and the world in which he lives.

But not so with Indian philosophy in any one of its six

56

forms, though one or two would seem to approach this purpose. Hindu philosophy has a very practical aim which has always been and is today to give men release from the burden of sorrow and suffering which is their lot in our world. Of the six systems which came into existence only one need occupy our attention in this study. It is the system of the Vedanta. The word "Vedanta" means the end, the purpose, or the outcome of the Veda, that to which the Vedas point as their ultimate goal. Building on the Upanishads, the Vedanta Sutras, and the Gita, three interpretations of the Vedanta came into existence, all of which have their advocates today. It must be said, however, that one of the interpretations has so far outdistanced the other two that it has become the prevailing philosophy of the land. The others have their advocates, but they form a tiny number as compared with those who adhere to the Vedanta of Shankara, which is known far and wide as "Indian philosophy." The three chief philosophers who wrote commentaries on the scriptures were Shankara, Ramanuja, and Madhva. It is of interest to know that while their views are known and accepted in every part of India, all three hail from the South and add to the pride of the people in that part of the country in their contribution to the development of Indian religion and philosophy.

Shankara's dates are not easy to determine. I shall not enter into the discussion, but merely state that by some he is thought to have lived sixty-two years (A.D. 788-850) and by others to have been but thirty-two when he died. At any rate Shankara did his work long years after the basic documents had been produced. But Hinduism had suffered greatly during the period of Buddhist ascendancy and had only recently passed through a revival period. A new day of power had arrived only a short time before Shankara lived and taught.

His interpretation of Vedanta is known as Advaita, or "nondualism." He was preceded by a thinker named Gaudapada, who was an uncompromising monist, an extreme view which Shankara found himself unable to accept. He could go along with his predecessor in believing that there was only one ultimate Reality, the Brahman of the *Upanishads*; but what was he to do when he faced the actual universe in which he lived with the thousand and one things about him, trees and mountains and other people, even his own body? He was sufficiently realistic to be unable to deny that they had some kind of existence, a fact which had been roundly denied by Gaudapada. And yet he could not be a dualist and give things a reality which had any likeness to the reality of Brahman. So he called his system "nondualism." He was a monist who could not go the entire distance traveled by the uncompromising Gaudapada. Shankara made use of the distinction between *seeming* reality and *actual* reality. What he saw about him in the physical universe did not really exist at all but had only a seeming existence.

Of course, this conclusion could not sustain itself in the mind of any consistent thinker without going a step, in fact, a number of steps, further. How came it that things had even a seeming existence? To this the answer was that it was because of our ignorance. We simply do not know the full meaning of reality; if we did, we would not make the fatal mistake of thinking that things existed when they really had only seeming existence. The fact is that the whole purpose of the Vedanta philosophy is to clarify our minds and make it possible to arrive at the insight which would pierce through our ignorance and help us to realize that seeming existences were seeming existences only and have no final actuality.

Only so much of Shankara's viewpoint is presented here as

will differentiate him from his later opponents. The teaching of Shankara is the orthodoxy of Hindu Vedantism and is the viewpoint which is to be set forth in the pages which follow. It will be well, however, to present briefly the views of the other two classical philosophers if for no other reason than to make the basic position of Shankara stand out the more clearly in contrast.

Ramanuja's dates are more certain than those of Shankara. He lived from A.D. 1050 to 1137, or over three centuries after his great predecessor. He is in the Vedantic tradition and looked upon the universe as a unity, as did Shankara; but there were modifications which made it into a much different kind of unity. He called his system "vishistadvaita"—it was nondualistic as was the Advaita of Shankara, but it was a "qualified nondualism." Rudolf Otto graphically contrasts the two systems:

For two magnitudes of the highest rank struggle here with each other in Shankara and Ramanuja, who are only their representatives. The almost altogether mysterious and overwhelming, world-destroying, ultimately irrational, unconceivable, undefinable absolute Unity is in conflict with the Lord, the feeling, willing, personal, rational, loving, and beloved God of the heart and conscience.[26]

Where we see the difference clearly is in Ramanuja's claim that there are three realities which unitedly make up the universe, and not one reality. God, the supreme, exists; but so do individual human beings as well as nonintelligent matter. We as men and women have real existence and freedom and are not doomed to lose our individuality in the Absolute. In fact the Absolute is a personal God with whom we are to enjoy personal fellowship in a real paradise to which human beings are destined ultimately to go. So different and antagonistic are

[26] *The Idea of the Holy*, p. 1.

the two systems that a prominent leader within the Hindu ranks in South India is recorded to have declared, "I would rather see all India become Christian than that it should fall a prey to the Vedanta of Shankara." [27] A most surprising statement that, but indicating that there are those in India today who take vigorous exception to Shankara.

If what has been said is true, how can Ramanuja be considered in the Vedanta tradition along with Shankara, whose views he opposed so strenuously? For the one reason that he posited a real unity. God, man, and nature were separate and distinct; but they belonged to one system and could not be thought of as existing separately and independently. Each was involved in the others, and all three were necessary in the constitution of a unified universe.

Ramanuja was, however, more than a philosopher. He was a deeply religious man and had the needs of religious people in mind in his thinking. His insistence on a real God, personal and alive to the needs of his worshipers, made his work the foundation of one of the most significant movements in the story of Hinduism. As Shankara stood for knowledge as the means of attaining the goal of human life, Ramanuja introduced a new era of deep devotional fervor. Out of his teachings came the bhakti movement. The closest English parallel to bhakti is given as "loving devotion." It differs from the Christian conception of faith but not greatly, especially when we think of Paul's phrase "faith working through love" (Gal. 5:6 R.S.V.). The bhakti movement was an appeal to the emotions and for centuries was the most prominent feature of Indian religious life. We have the names and sayings of a score and more of ecstatic singers who in some cases reached high stages

---

[27] Schomerus, *Der Shaiva Siddhanta*, p. 20.

of religious attainment. Unfortunately, while the bhakti attitude remains an impressive phase of Hinduism, its glory lies in the past. The belief in a personal God, which is an essential ingredient in the bhakti attitude, has had a hard time of it in India. In the running battle which it has always had to fight with the Vedanta of Shankara and his successors, it has been worsted by its opponents. Today the exponent of the Vedanta who is known in the Western world is always a believer in Brahman, the impersonal All, in whom all men are to lose identity when the illusion of separate existence has finally been shaken off.

The third of the classical philosophers is Madhva, whose probable dates are A.D. 1199 to 1278. He is far less known than his two predecessors, books of only a few years ago passing him by with only a brief reference. It is significant that M. Hiriyanna should not have mentioned Madhva in his earlier volume *Outlines of Indian Philosophy*, while in his more recent book *The Essentials of Indian Philosophy* (1949) there is a short but satisfactory presentation. This thinker went further than Ramanuja in his opposition to the cardinal factors in the system of Shankara. He did not believe, as did Ramanuja, that God is embodied in individual souls and in matter even though they are to be carefully distinguished. His idea was that God in his majesty is a completely transcendent being, "high and lifted up," as was the Lord in Isaiah's vision. He held to the doctrine of Bheda, or "difference," as fundamental. God is God and man is man, and they are placed opposite to each other, God as Creator and man as creature. God is the only one in the universe who is absolutely independent as Creator and Sustainer of all that is. His system has received the name "dvaita," which means undiluted "dualism." The final source of attaining salvation is God's love, or grace. Many if not all of these statements have a Christian ring and demonstrate the hidden possibilities of the Hindu heart and mind. The kind of gospel which Paul preached does find in the Indian mind a point of contact, at the present time almost completely engrossed by the prevailing philosophy, the Vedanta of Shankara.

With this background we may take up step by step the various aspects of the Vedanta and see them in contrast with the teachings and attitudes coming out of the Christian gospel. But as a preliminary step it seems well to consider the Vedantic attitude toward history in contrast to the Christian attitude. That attitude colors much of Hindu thinking and is determinative of a number of ideas which make up what we know as Vedantic Hinduism.

Chapter Three

Why Bother with History?

I<small>T</small> is a common saying among Vedantists and others who
are like-minded that it makes no difference whether Rama or
Krishna or Christ ever lived or not; we may profit by what they
are reported to have taught, but this has nothing to do with
the question of their actual existence as historical characters.
This is one aspect of the strange apathy to history which has
characterized the writers and thinkers of India from the earliest
time almost to the present day. Within the last century Indian historians have come to the fore with historical writings
which are highly creditable and enriching. This new direction
which Indian scholarship has been taking brings into even
stronger light the dearth of historical thought and writing in
the past. In no sense does this devaluate the wealth of the Indian literary product through the centuries. Indians have produced a remarkable literature, various items of which stand out
as masterpieces. There are religious lyrics, great epic narra-
tives, notable philosophical treatises, and manuals of devotion
and conduct of life, not to mention other works which are
the product of the Indian literary genius—but no histories or
even chronologies.

The first verifiable date in Indian history is the year 326 B.C.,
when Alexander the Great invaded the land. The Greeks were
historians—has not Herodotus been called the "Father of
History"? We cannot be sure of the dates of Gautama Buddha,
the greatest personality India has ever produced. Probably the

best estimate is that he lived from 563 to 483 B.C. The only way we have of being sure of events and dates between A.D. 400 and 700 is from the writings of Chinese Buddhist pilgrims who visited India and wrote accounts of their journeys and of conditions as they observed them. These are the only trustworthy sources to which Indian historians have access for these centuries. The Mohammedans began their incursions into India about A.D. 1000, when the Afghan freebooter Mahmud of Ghazni made the first of seventeen forays into the peninsula from the northwest. Like the Greeks and the Chinese, the Muslims have kept records and written histories. The same is true of the Portuguese, who first arrived on the southwest coast of India in 1498, and also of course of the French and British. The Hindus stand out in striking contrast. We are dealing with a unique phenomenon, a people who have little or no sense of the meaning of time and its passage, who have not seen any reason why they should set down in writing a record of the events which are taking place either for themselves or for generations yet to be born. We can easily imagine an Indian saying, "We are interested in the eternal and spiritual, not in the temporal and material; the outward events are of little significance—they are not worth recording."

A statement of this position is to be found in *Vedanta for Modern Man* (1951) in a chapter on "A Hindu View of Christian Theology," by Swami Siddheswarananda, head of the French Vedanta center at Gratz. He writes:

The process of fulfillment in time, and an absolute value given to history—essential to the Christian because of the Judaic notion of the static quality of time—are not articles of faith in India. When Ramakrishna was told of the doubts of the modern educated mind as to the historicity of Krishna, he replied that the fact that Lord Krishna expresses himself in the lives of mystics and devotees is incontrovertible evidence of his existence! The existence of a birth certificate for a spiritual hero does not give him any greater efficacy than that which mythology has awarded.[1]

And again from the same author:

Spiritual personalities like Rama and Krishna get out of the framework of history and really treat the soul that is sick and regenerate it into spiritual glory. They remain as the very salt of the earth. Mahatma Gandhi prayed to Rama and through repeating the name of Rama he got the power to awaken the masses of India.[2]

It will not be out of place to mention another movement, namely, the Zen sect of Buddhism in Japan, which has precisely the same attitude toward history as the Vedanta. D. T. Suzuki, the chief exponent of Zen for Western readers, has this to say:

What is history? What is a historical personage? Shall we regard this sense-world, time-divided, as more real, dependable, and trustworthy than the spiritual one which transcends limitations of time and space? Is the spiritual world just a fabrication of a visionary, that is, untrustworthy mind? Is the year 1946 really more real than the year zero, or time beyond measurement, for instance, "infinite Kalpas ago"? [3]

What are these men telling us? On even a cursory reading it is plain that they look on history and historical evidence as unnecessary in religion and religious living. They would agree with the philosopher Lessing that the contingent facts of history are insufficient to establish the eternal truths of religion. That is, to the Vedantist an intuition, a spiritual illumination,

---

[1] Pp. 314-15. Christopher Isherwood, ed. Used by permission of Harper & Bros.
[2] Ibid., p. 315.
[3] The Essence of Buddhism, pp. 71-72.

an immediate awareness or cognition of truth with no reference to things that have taken place in historic time, uncontrolled by reason and reasoning processes, such an intuition is a sufficient foundation on which to build religious belief and practice. Whatever we may say of the value of intuition, we must ever keep in mind that it does not convey factual knowledge of the world outside the human mind. It has its place in providing illumination and insight into the meaning and significance of religious experience. In this we are in agreement with the Vedantic mystic and devotee, but he would have us go further and accept his belief that all that a religious man needs is provided by this immediate awareness, this spiritual illumination. By intuition we may be sure of the reality of a spiritual world, but the question is, Is that all that is necessary? Does it matter whether Rama or Krishna or Christ ever lived or not? And the emphatic answer of the Hindu is that it does not. Yet it is a strange claim that spiritual intuition gives "incontrovertible evidence of his [Krishna's] existence!" to use the words of Sri Ramakrishna in the first of the quotations above. Why should "evidence of his existence" be needed if it makes no difference whether he ever lived or not? Krishna is an object of devotion outside the mind of the devotee. Where did the name and idea of Krishna come from except out of traditions of the past? One comes perilously near asserting his dependence on history while declaring that history and the time process have no necessary connection with religious experience. While these assertions do not seem reasonable to us whose entire background is so different, we are bound to take the Hindu as he is and try to realize what the difference between us means.

To state the issue at once and very sharply, nothing could be more contrary to virtually unanimous Christian conviction than the Hindu attitude toward history and time. We have been taught that Christianity is a historical religion and that it would evaporate and cease to be were it not rooted and grounded in historical fact, in events which actually took place at a definite place on our planet and at an ascertainable time in world history.

To put the problem concretely, we may institute several comparisons. Does it make any difference whether Shakespeare's Hamlet or the Alice of Lewis Carroll's *Alice's Adventures in Wonderland* ever lived or not? Not the slightest, and the fact that they are imaginary characters does not stand in the way of the enjoyment and profit we may secure from what Shakespeare and Lewis Carroll have created out of their imagination. But let us ask another question, this time of an Indian. Does it make any difference whether Mohandas Gandhi ever lived or not? And the only possible answer is that it makes a world of difference. But why in this case and not in that of Hamlet and Alice in Wonderland? One can see on a moment's thought that Gandhi did something which gave a new direction to Indian history. Had he not lived and performed the remarkable service which he rendered, no one knows when India would have become free. It would undoubtedly have been achieved in time, but India would be very different today had Gandhi not worked for a half century to bring about independence. No wonder he is called the Father of Indian Independence. Every American knows that, had it not been for George Washington, the Revolution might have failed. It was he more than anyone else who kept up the courage of the patriots and who did not falter during the period when the fortunes of the nation that was being born were at a very low ebb. He performed an inestimable service so that he earned the title of the Father of his Country—he had done something which makes a difference for us Americans today. Every Negro in America knows that his freedom was achieved because of the bold step taken by Abraham Lincoln when he signed the Emancipation Proclamation. His act and the conviction back of it made him the Great Emancipator. It is such deeds which have made history and cause us to honor the names of those through whom came to us the blessings we enjoy.

So we come back to Rama and Krishna and Christ. I can understand the Indian who says that it makes no difference whether Rama or Krishna ever lived or not. They are the two most important avatars, or incarnations of the great god Vishnu; they have become so important that, almost forgetting Vishnu, they are worshiped in their own right in countless shrines and temples all over the land. In the *Gita*, Krishna, the more important of the two, declares himself to be the Supreme Being. Equivalent not only to Vishnu, he is raised to the pinnacle where he could justifiably be adored as Brahman, the Absolute All, the final reality in this universe of ours. And yet it makes no difference whether Krishna or Rama ever lived or not. Many things are placed to their credit in the great Indian epics. Rama is the hero in the epic *Ramayana*, where his exploits and experiences are recounted so that they have become the fireside tales of millions of people. In the *Gita*, Krishna is the counselor of Arjuna, the prince of the Pandavas, who is the general on one side in the fabled battle of Kurukshetra. The popular poem the *Mahabharata* is the longest in all the world's literature, and the *Bhagavad-Gita* (*Gita*) is an episode in one of its earlier sections. These characters have an established place in the esteem and love of Hindus high and low.

With all that might be said about Rama and Krishna the question arises, How much of what is recounted about them and their character is true to fact? The *Ramayana* and the *Mahabharata* are for the most part imaginary. Was the battle of Kurukshetra ever fought; is the quarrel between the Pandavas and the Kurus more than fiction? There are many Hindu fundamentalists who would have us believe that every event recorded in the epics is true, but many could not go as far as that. There are all too many wonders to allow the modern scientific Hindu historian to assert the historicity of much that is to be found in these writings. I was invited to attend a meeting of the Arya Samaj on the occasion of the alleged birthday of Krishna. Much of what was said in Hindi was translated quietly to me as one speaker after another told of Krishna, that he was a great hero, a great counselor, a great ruler and administrator, and so on through other characterizations, with not the slightest question being raised as to whether all the statements made or any of them could be substantiated by adequate historical evidence. The fact is that the whole story of Krishna is based so largely on imaginative legend, bordering on myth, that it is difficult to extract the modicum of reliable fact in any part of the narrative. What this amounts to is that no one knows what the real Krishna was like or even if there ever was such a character. The one great significant fact is that Krishna—and the same may be said of Rama—cannot justifiably be said to have performed a single act which makes the slightest difference in the life of anyone living today. No wonder a Hindu can say with no fear of contradiction that it makes no difference whether Krishna or Rama ever lived or not.

It is essential for the Christian believer to realize the significance of history and historical events in his religion. One of the great contributions of William Temple, the late Archbishop of Canterbury, in his Gifford Lectures is his insistence on the supreme importance of history, especially in its relation to the revelation of God as we have it in the Bible. The reading of this volume, *Nature, Man and God*, began for me a new era in my thinking concerning the nature of revelation. God reveals himself and his will in the universe by reason of the fact that he created it and sustains it continuously. He also reveals himself in the special acts of his providence and grace in the events of human history. This might be said to be the theme of the Old Testament. God made himself known through his "mighty acts unto the children of Israel," not only in the sublime act of rescuing them from slavery in the land of Egypt but through all their subsequent history. The great function of the prophetic writers was to see the meaning of these acts and interpret them to the people. In that was their inspiration; they were divinely gifted seers who were enabled to penetrate deeply into the mind of God and declare the message of the Almighty to a people often reluctant to hear and heed. So the revelation was not a book, though the Bible contains the record of the revelation; it was not in words and doctrines conveyed by dictation from above; it was rather in the acts of God interpreted by men who were so close to God that they saw meanings in events which were entirely opaque to the populace. As William Temple puts it, "The typical *locus* of revelation is not the mind of the seer but the historical event." And again, "The prophet is enabled to interpret the circumstance as it falls within the divine purpose; in other words, we have here the perfect example of revelation—divinely guided external event interpreted by a mind divinely illuminated to that end." [4]

If this is true in respect of the Old Testament, how much more so of the New. The life of Christ is so firmly attached to history that mankind as a whole and the Christian world in particular join in an almost unanimous chorus in declaring

[4] Pp. 318, 341.

that his life was the most influential in human history. A person who actually lived is the only explanation of the influences which have emanated from him and of the direction he has given to the story of our race. We must penetrate, however, to a deeper level than this. Far more than in the case of Gandhi and his relation to Indian freedom and of Abraham Lincoln to the emancipation of the Negro, Jesus Christ did something for mankind. We may study his message in his life, his teachings, his attitudes, his conduct in all sorts of relations with his fellow countrymen; but everything comes to a supreme climax in his death on the cross and in his resurrection from the dead which followed on the third day after. The Christian gospel centers in the act of God who sent his only begotten Son into our world in order to bring salvation to mankind. Were it not for this deed which happened at a definite place on our planet and at a definite time in human history, Christianity would be without its distinctive message, its gospel of salvation from sin, and the assurance of its promise of eternal life. So it is a life and death matter for our religion as to whether history is real and time is significant. We hear the apostle Paul saying, "But when the time had fully come, God sent forth his Son" (Gal. 4:4 R.S.V.). That reference to time is and must be characteristic of Christianity.

So important is the relation of our religion to history and time that the most important part of the New Testament, the four Gospels, was written to make sure that it would never be forgotten that Jesus Christ actually lived among men. We must realize the significance of Ernest F. Scott's weighty little volume *The Purpose of the Gospels* where he says, "For other religions the trust in God can never be much more than a sublime conjecture." In contrast he declares that "the aim of the Gospels, therefore, is to place the Christian beliefs on a ground of certainty." We might say that the Gospels are like the announcement of a herald making it known that the most important event in the history of the world had taken place.[5]

This would not be the place to enter into a discussion of the historicity of the life of Jesus, even if I were competent to make an authoritative statement. Not being a specialist in New Testament criticism, I am compelled to reach a decision on this matter by accepting the verdict of those whom I feel I can trust. But do not even first-rate critics differ in their conclusions? Of course they do, and at times it is quite disconcerting. But real advances have been made. The theory propounded a half century ago by a few extremists that Jesus never lived at all is completely discredited today. There were those who were very sure a few years ago that, on the basis of the conclusions reached by certain advocates of form criticism of the Gospels, we could make few if any statements about the life and teachings of Jesus of which we could be certain. These extreme views, however, are at a discount today; and the world of Christian scholarship is coming to a deeper confidence that we can know the main facts concerning the life of our Lord and may use the Gospels with the assurance that we are in intimate contact with him and his message. Many years ago James Denney declared that the Gospels disclose a person "who is not only equal to the place which Christian faith assigns Him but who assumes that place naturally and spontaneously as His own." Of these words Archibald M. Hunter says in his *Interpreting the New Testament*, "After forty years that argument [of Denney's] remains as clear and strong and convincing as ever." [6] We hear Vincent Taylor declaring at the close of *The Gospel*

[5] Pp. 155, 89, 44.
[6] P. 51.

According to St. Mark, the latest authoritative discussion (1952) of this Gospel: "In sum we may say that in Mark we have an authority of first rank for our knowledge of the story of Jesus." [7] We proceed on the basis that that conclusion is valid and can be depended on.

Like ourselves the Hindu lives in the succession of events which is called time, but it has little or no meaning for him. He can see no purpose or aim being worked out in the process. Time has no beginning and no end, so it is said; so it does not seem quite consistent that he should hold the belief in what he calls Kalpas, or ages of the world, enormously long eons of time between one period of utter chaos and nothingness and the next. How long is a Kalpa? No exact calculations are of course possible, but it would not be exaggerating to say that each Kalpa extends over millions of years. Indian writers have a number of picturesque ways of trying to make such a prodigious expanse of time understandable to the common man. Imagine a mountain of solid rock out in the middle of a plain; also imagine that a drop of water falls on this great rock mountain every hour; how long would it take for the water to wear the mountain down until it is level with the plain? Well, that is a Kalpa. Then follows an approximately equally long period of chaos, which again is succeeded by another Kalpa. The important point to be made is that there is no progress, no purpose being worked out, no intelligible goal which can fill the mind of man with a hope of something better and more permanent. There is a real likeness between this Hindu conception and that of the Greeks of the classical period. They believed in a series of ages of the world, or cycles, which never reached a terminus or desirable end, but consisted of endless repetition with no purpose being worked out and no variation in the pattern.

Time is a problem which has exercised the minds of thinkers from the earliest days of recorded thought. A considerable amount of writing has been done by Christian theologians who have differed from one another on the question of time and eternity, on God's purpose in the times in which men live on this planet and its relation to eternity "when time shall be no more," as one school phrases its thought. A very significant contribution has been made by Oscar Cullmann in his volume *Christ and Time.*[8] Time does not run in cycles, as in the thought of the Greeks, but is better represented by a straight line which starts with God's creation of the universe and ends with the Parousia, the close of the earthly era which began with the creation. There is also what Cullmann calls the "mid-point," which is that of Jesus Christ and his death and resurrection. This is the climactic point in world history, to which all that came before pointed in the story of the "redemptive history" and from which every event takes its significance and will continue to take its meaning until the end of human history. More than that, the period before creation and that after the Parousia is not timeless eternity but endless time. This conception makes eternity fall into the time scheme, not something utterly at variance with time and its succession of events as we know it. This thesis is developed at length as the real meaning of the concept of time in both the Old and New Testaments. God has a purpose, and it is being worked out in time. Tennyson, coming out of the Christian tradition, caught this biblical note in the familiar words "Yet I doubt not through the ages one increasing purpose runs," [9] and in the even more familiar lines

[8] Tr. Floyd V. Filson.
[9] *Locksley Hall*, l. 137.

And one far-off divine event,
To which the whole creation moves.[10]

Whether we are in accord with every feature of Cullmann's argument or not, we must agree that he has made an important contribution, that he has shown conclusively that the concept of time, as inextricably bound up with the Christian idea of creation and of redemption, is an inescapable fact.

At the Indian Philosophical Congress Silver Jubilee Session, held in Calcutta in 1950, John F. Butler, formerly professor of philosophy in the Madras Christian College, read a paper entitled *Faith, Hope, and Love in the Christian Apprehension of God in Time*. Speaking as he did before an audience of distinguished Indian philosophers, his words came with more weight as the expression of the Christian viewpoint and in strong contrast with the convictions of the many Hindu scholars present:

The clauses in the Apostles' Creed teach, not primarily that God is a *saving* God, but that God, in the governorship of Pontius Pilate in Judaea, *has wrought salvation*. The redemptiveness of God could have been taught, in principle, by anyone: it has, in fact, been taught by many, including many non-Christians: it is the claim made for the existence and unique significance of a particular set of historical facts that makes the distinctiveness. To put it in another way, the Sermon on the Mount, if true, would still be true even if Christ were proved to be, as some extremists would have Him, a sun-myth; likewise the *Gita*, if true theology and ethics, is still such even if its historical setting in the *Mahabharata* be taken as pure fiction: but, without a historical, factual life, death and resurrection of Jesus Christ Christianity as such would collapse; it is concerned mainly to proclaim not that Jesus' way of life was a good one or that God is, practically speaking, like Jesus, but that in

[10] *In Memoriam*, st. 36.

Jesus Christ certain decisive and unique acts of salvation were wrought.[11]

So, to conclude, it may not make any difference whether Rama or Krishna ever lived or not, but it makes all the difference in the world whether Christ ever lived or not. History counts; time is real; our very salvation depends upon events which took place in time and are a part of recorded history. We cannot have it both ways; either time and history are significant, or they are not. The choice must be made.

---

[11] *Indian Philosophical Congress Silver Jubilee Commemorative Volume*, I, 193. Used by permission.

Chapter Four

Ultimate Reality and the Universe

THE ultimate reality in Christianity is God the Father of our Lord Jesus Christ. He is a personal God who enters into relations with human beings, hearing and answering their prayers. He is the all-wise and almighty one who created and sustains the universe by the word of his power. He is altogether righteous and demands righteousness of his human creatures. God is love and in his infinite tenderness and mercy forgives his people for their evil doings when they come to him in sorrow and penitence. And this God revealed himself to men in Jesus Christ his Son, our Savior and Lord. He is present with us now through the Holy Spirit, a living reality in the experience of his people. These are the fundamental affirmations which all Christians make when they testify to their belief. They are stated here as a background against which to consider the nature of ultimate reality as held by all those who adhere to the Vedanta philosophy, however they may differ at this point or that in minor details.

In the Vedanta the ultimate reality is Brahman, the Absolute, the All, everything that exists. Since Brahman includes all that exists, since Brahman is the entire universe and the universe is Brahman, the system of which this is the primary and all-inclusive affirmation has been called a pantheism and a monism—which is the preferable designation? When a system of thought or a world view is spoken of as a pantheism, the implication is that there is a God—the word "theism" indicates that—but according to the Vedanta the conception of a being who has any likeness to the deities in other religions is not consistent with the idea of ultimate reality. So while the word "pantheism" is frequently used of the Vedantic conception of the final reality, it would seem more fitting to think of the Vedanta as a monism; for by using that designation no assertion is made, one way or another, about a divine being, a cosmos, or anything else. All that is indicated is that ultimate reality is bare, simple unity; and that is very close to what a Vedantist means when he thinks of Brahman.[1]

What then can be said of Brahman? We are told over and over again that Brahman is "attributeless," that no positive affirmation can be made, except of course that there is an entity called Brahman. In the words of Swami Nikhilananda, "All that can be said, then, of Brahman is that It is." [2] Note the neuter pronoun "It" used by this Vedantist writer. Brahman is often referred to as "He"; but this writer holds, it would seem rightly, that in speaking of the attributeless Brahman the proper term is "It." Of It nothing can be known, and the answer to every question can only be *neti, neti,* "not this, not this," or as often used, "not that, not that." It is completely unknowable, to be referred to in negative terms only. Many such negative statements are to be found in the *Upanishads.* For example, in the *Brihadaranyaka Upanishad* (3.8.8.) a long itemized list of negatives is given. The following is a selection of these items: "It is not coarse, not fine, not short, not long, not glowing, not adhesive, without shadow and without darkness . . . odorless, tasteless, without eye, without ear, without voice, without mind, without energy . . . without personal or

---

[1] For discussion of these terms see M. H. Harrison, *Hindu Monism and Pluralism,* pp. 91, 129-30.

[2] *Op. cit.,* I, 33.

family name, unageing, undying, without fear, immortal, stainless. . . . It consumes nothing soever. No one soever consumes it." [3] In the *Mandukya Upanishad* (1.1.6) we find this: "That which is invisible, ungraspable, without family, without caste—without sight or hearing is It, without hand or foot, eternal." [4] Hume adds, "He is apart from all moral, causal, or temporal relations. . . . 'Indefinable,' 'inconceivable,' mere negative statements are all that can be asserted of this pure being, which *ex hypothesi* is incapable of the qualification, determination, and diversity implied in descriptive attribution." [5]

In spite of the vigorous assertion, often repeated, that Brahman is attributeless, we are told that It has existence (sat), consciousness (chit), and bliss (ananda). These terms are to be found as early as the *Upanishads* and become of high importance in later writers. They have caused considerable difficulty among Vedantists themselves. There are those who cannot see how these descriptive terms, positive in character, can be attached to Brahman, the Brahman who is attributeless and cannot be described or defined. It is quite evident that "existence" might be asserted of a being without attributes, the bare truth that such an entity exists. But when it comes to "consciousness" and "bliss," these are surely descriptive terms, attributes, or qualities. But Swami Nikhilananda will have it otherwise. To him "Sat, Chit, and Anandam can very well refer to the attributeless Brahman; for these words are used, it is declared, in a negative sense. Sat indicates that Brahman is not nonbeing; Chit, that Brahman is not nescient; and Anandam, that Brahman is not a mere absence of pain. By such denial the positive nature of Brahman as the Absolute is affirmed." Also

---

[3] Hume, *op. cit.*, p. 39. Used by permission of Oxford University Press.
[4] *Ibid.*
[5] *Ibid.*, pp. 39-40.

the following: "Existence, Consciousness, and Bliss—then, are not attributes of Brahman, but Its very essence. Brahman is not endowed with them: Brahman is Existence itself, Consciousness itself, and Bliss itself. In the Absolute there is no distinction between substance and attributes." [6] It is difficult if not impossible to avoid the thought that we are here being introduced to a distinction without a difference. Consciousness and bliss certainly look like qualities or attributes, so much so that we find ourselves on the side of those who believe they are. However the idea is interpreted, it is evident that the Hindu finds it difficult to think of Brahman wholly without attributes.

Vedantists no more than ourselves can live for very long in such a rarefied atmosphere, so completely out of contact with the material world and with their fellow human beings. So we discover that very early the idea that there are two Brahmans begins to emerge, *Nirguna* Brahman, or the Brahman *without* attributes, with which we have just been dealing; and *Saguna* Brahman, or the Brahman *with* attributes. The *Nirguna* Brahman, spoken of as the noumenal or transcendental Brahman, is the real Brahman, which has existence and of which it can be said that "It is." On the other hand, the *Saguna* Brahman, the phenomenal, has attributes and qualities. He is a Being with whom we can have dealings. But in the final analysis he is unreal and does not really exist at all. And yet this unreal reality includes the universe in which we live and move and have our being; it is the world of material things, the universe. In fact it includes ourselves as personal beings when we think of them as separate, independent entities in themselves. It also includes all the deities which have ever been worshiped anywhere in the world and all the priesthoods and paraphernalia of religion. The

* Op. cit., I, 36-37. Used by permission of Harper & Bros.

sweep is all-inclusive when we think of things and people as entities having a real existence.

How can all this be? How can all that occupies the human mind, such as ideas and purposes and aspirations, come into being, even as thoughts, if the all-embracing Brahman is the only entity that exists? Brahman is declared not to have thoughts or purposes or anything else which might make possible even a seeming world. Here we come to one of the strangest conceptions which has entered the mind of man. The fact, already stated, is that Shankara, the greatest of the Vedantists, found he could not be an absolute monist. He was too conscious of the world of things and people around him to be able to say that they did not exist at all, even though he might think of them as unreal. So he borrowed a conception which is to be found in the *Upanishads* and made it of the highest importance in his system, the conception expressed by the word "maya." It would take us too far afield to attempt a complete discussion of an idea which is so far-reaching and has had so many interpretations as maya. Even today there is no unanimity in the definitions and explanations which are being given. Reference may be made to a comprehensive study in the volume entitled *The Concept of Maya* by P. D. Devanandan, an Indian Christian scholar, who as a student of the original sources has earned the right to an opinion which must be taken into account by Vedantists and non-Vedantists alike.

As a broad generalization it may be said that maya is that which is accountable for the universe as distinct from the one final reality, the attributeless Brahman. Where did the word itself, "maya," come from? There is no agreement even at this point. Is it derived from the Aryan invaders whose language, the Sanskrit, is the most important source of India's religious vocabulary? Or was it one of the contributions made

81

to Hinduism by the Dravidians, whom the Aryans encountered as they advanced into the country? These contributions are far more numerous and important than scholars recognized a half or even a quarter of a century ago. Not only so, but the word has had a history and a development. Devanandan shows that one of the early connotations was that of "power," but it is a peculiar kind of power. Early in Indian religious history the idea of "shakti" comes into prominence. Shakti means power or energy, but it is the energy of a female consort of one of the divinities. "The 'sakti' concept has been universalized and personalized in Kali. Kali is the maha [great] Maya, the Goddess of Primal Energy. The very name Maya is retained, and henceforth it is equivalent to the 'power' of God, of God Himself as actively directing the affairs of man." [7]

The primary form in which Brahman is related to the world under the influence of maya is that of Isvara, who appears as the creator God responsible for the world, for the entire universe. Of course it must be understood that Isvara is not real any more than anything else in the phenomenal universe. Let us not forget that all the way through the Vedantic theory of reality is an unreal world and an unknowable reality, Brahman. But Shankara could not deny that there was a universe of some kind. According to his theory it could only be unreal, unless one should do what he actually did, posit a phenomenal world alongside the only real existence, the Absolute. Was he not a living human being in contact with other human beings and dependent for his very life on material food and drink? This fact was so strongly borne in upon Shankara that it made it impossible to follow his predecessor Gaudapada, who was as near to being an absolute monist as a man could be. But Gaudapada

[7] The Concept of Maya, p. 226. Used by permission of Lutterworth Press.

held that the world "can be understood only when it is completely denied." [8] Shankara did not go as far as that; he could not go to the point of denying that the universe had some kind of existence. The result was that he called his system not monism but "nondualism" (Advaita). By using this negative way of stating his position Shankara lets it be known that something other than Brahman lies in his mind even though he cannot assert its real existence. It is hard to escape the thought that Shankara is attempting to carry water on both shoulders and in the end finds it impossible. So his final position is that the universe which he would like to think of as more than an imaginary thing is in reality only an illusion, that Brahman is the only entity with real existence.

There is that word "illusion"; is it a true description of what is being discussed? It is hard to avoid the conclusion that the phenomenal world is an illusion—we think it exists, but it doesn't. Maya itself is frequently called an illusion, but there is more to it than the word "illusion" usually signifies. Maya is looked upon more as a power, to go back to its very early connotation, or a force which produces the illusion. To go a step further, maya is the power of ignorance, a not-knowing what the final reality Brahman is and involves. And yet, of course, it is not a conscious force and it is only a seeming reality, and this makes more reasonable the idea that maya might justifiably be called an illusion. But this unreal power is responsible for all that seems to exist, and it has certainly had a magnificent and mighty part to play in the whole scheme of things as we know it. But, says Swami Nikhilananda, "Maya and its manifestations disappear with the dawn of the Knowledge of Brahman." [9]

Hindus are aware of the baffling nature of the concept of

[8] W. S. Urquhart, *The Vedanta and Modern Thought*, p. 48.
[9] *Op. cit.*, I, 56.

maya. Radhakrishnan finds the problem insoluble: "The word 'maya' registers our finiteness and points to a gap in our knowledge." He quotes Deussen as saying, "How do we manage to deceive ourselves into seeing a transformation and a plurality, where in reality Brahman alone is? On this question our authors give no information," and then Radhakrishnan adds the significant sentence, "They give us no information, simply because 'no information' is possible." [10]

This illusion, in the toils of which we live, is of course ours as individuals with minds which can function for themselves; but it is more than that; there is a cosmic illusion which enshrouds all there is. The cosmos seems to us to be real, but it is just as completely tied up with maya as we are and so is illusory. In the words of Swami Nikhilananda:

Maya generally signifies the cosmic illusion on account of which Brahman, or Pure Consciousness, appears as the Creator, Preserver, and Destroyer of the universe. . . . Maya, both in its cosmic and in its individual aspect, hides the true nature of Brahman. Thus it becomes the upadhi, or limiting adjunct, of Brahman. But the infinite Brahman can never be limited; therefore this limitation is only apparent, and not real.

Though not real, Saguna Brahman, with attributes, comes to be known as Isvara, the "all-powerful, the Lord of all, the Ruler of the entire universe." [11] He controls the universe, the sun, the moon, and the stars; he is also in control of the moral power to be found in the universe and in the life of the individual man. Isvara takes the place which is assigned to God in the Judaeo-Christian scriptures in respect of his relation to nature and the moral life of mankind. Isvara is said to be worshiped

[10] The Vedanta, pp. 135, 144.
[11] Op. cit., I, 57, 60.

in all the deities of India and also in the person of the Allah of the Muslims, Ahura Mazda of the Zoroastrians, and the God of the Old and New Testaments. But again it must be repeated that these are all unreal, including Isvara himself. How easy then it is for Vedantists to declare that it makes no difference what god a man may worship—are they not all ultimately unreal, all except the attributeless, inscrutable, unknowable Brahman? Yes, the universe, the world of men and all that concerns their lives, has meant much to Shankara and his successors to the present day; but their primary intuition, their underlying conviction, was an effective barrier, preventing them from giving the created world of things and men the dignity of reality.

Often in India one sees a little brass image of the Sanskrit character or syllable Om (also spelled Aum). At its base is a little cup for oil to feed a lighted taper; the image is also fitted with small openings for sticks of incense, aids to the worship of the syllable itself. Now Om is not only the symbol of Brahman: Om *is* Brahman. In the words of the *Katha Upanishad,* "The goal which all the Vedas declare, which all austerities aim at, and which men desire when they lead the life of continence, I will tell you briefly: it is Om. This syllable Om is indeed Brahman. This syllable is the Highest. . . . Who so knows this support is adored in the world of Brahma." [12] The last word, "Brahma," is not the same as Brahman; he is the Saguna Brahman, the Brahman with attributes, and is equated with Isvara. And yet in the quotation just given this lesser Brahma is in close relations with Brahman, the Absolute. The writer of the *Katha Upanishad* believes in Brahman, the Absolute; yet Brahma, who belongs to the world which is unreal, has a certain kind of reality. In this *Upanishad* there is a strong theistic

[12] *Ibid.,* p. 75.

85

trend, which illustrates the fact that the Indian heart craves a personal God; but this craving is hard put to it by the glacier-like power of the other trend, that toward belief in one and only one reality, Brahman the Absolute, a trend which has almost always won its way to acceptance and has become the typical attitude of the Indian mind.

We now face a question of high importance and yet one which is as nearly unanswerable as it can be. Some simply throw it over as altogether beyond our ken as human beings. Why should there be a phenomenal world at all? It came into such existence as it has out of ignorance—cosmic ignorance, whatever that may mean. To quote Urquhart, "The cosmic ignorance when combined with power becomes a principle of illusion or Maya," which "somehow or other . . . become attached to the ultimate Being, Brahman. It is an eternal power producing unreal appearances." [13] He quotes from Radhakrishnan, who says, "As for the metaphysical ramifications which also exist, the non-dualist says, well, they are there, and there is an end of it. We do not know and cannot know why. It is all a contradiction and yet it is actual." [14] With all that, Urquhart is convinced that the "conception of Maya does afford us some relief from the burden of the inexplicable." [15]

We must not think that all Hindus, not even all Vedantists, have been carried by these extreme views. We have in Ramanuja a sage and a scholar who disagrees completely with his more famous predecessor, Shankara. Could there be more violent disagreement than that expressed in the following words?

This entire theory rests on a fictitious foundation of altogether hollow and vicious arguments, incapable of being stated in definite

[13] Op. cit., p. 57.
[14] History of Indian Philosophy, I, 35.
[15] Op. cit., p. 57.

logical alternatives, and devised by men who are destitute of those particular qualities which cause individuals to be chosen by the Supreme Person revealed in the Upanishads; whose intellects are darkened by the impression of beginningless evils and who have thus no insight into the meaning of words and sentences, into the real purport conveyed by them, and into the procedure of sound argumentation. . . . The theory therefore must needs be rejected by all those, who, through texts, perception, and other means of knowledge—assisted by sound reasoning—have an insight into the true nature of things.[16]

Ramanuja felt that he was in the presence of a god of love, a god who was a being with personal qualities, above or with whom there was no superior inscrutable being whom no one could know and who did not enter into the lives of men. And yet Shankara won the victory; and while Ramanuja has his following today, the typical Indian intellectual is convinced that Shankara was right and not Ramanuja. The Vedanta as expounded by Shankara is the philosophy which is thought of as truly Indian and is the doctrine which is now being carried to other lands.

Shankara's commentaries on the *Upanishads*, the *Vedanta Sutras*, and the *Bhagavad-Gita* are those most commonly referred to by Indian students. They seek to prove that the burden of all these classics is monistic and that they do not allow a theistic interpretation despite passage after passage which would seem not only to warrant but to demand such an interpretation.[17] The Ramakrishna Mission, following its founder, Swami Vivekananda, has gone the entire distance and accepted Shankara as mentor in their teaching. We need only give a typical testimony, that of C. N. K. Aiyer, "It was given to Shankara

[16] Max Muller, ed., *Sacred Books of the East*, tr. and introduced by G. Buhler, XLVIII, 8. Used by permission of Oxford University Press.
[17] See, for example, Rawson, op. cit., passim, as well as Hume, op. cit., Intro. and notes.

to make Vedanta the basis of every religious sect that India has known, so as to satisfy the needs of men of all shades of intelligence and bias." [18]

We have another question to answer: Whence did maya arise? How account for the emergence of this power, illusive and nescient, which yet has had such a momentous part to play in the universe and in human life? If Brahman, the attributeless, is all there is of reality, is it possible to escape the conclusion that maya must have its origin in that which is all that exists? Whence otherwise could it have come into such existence as it has? Indian and Western scholars have seen no other valid— if this can be called valid—explanation. But such a conclusion at once plunges us into an intellectual predicament: How can an absolutely self-sufficient being, an entity complete, wanting and needing nothing, which can neither think or desire—in any sense which the human mind can fathom—which cannot look into the future and make plans—how can such a being be conceived of as doing anything whatsoever? The fundamental possibility of a motive is wanting. Brahman has no reason for doing anything. It is all that exists, and nothing can be added to what is already all-inclusive and perfect. The Indian thinker has been driven to make use of the idea of Lila, or "sport," an unmotivated act which is done without any meaning or significance, "just for fun," if such a phrase may be allowed. The example which has been used is that of a typical Indian rajah of the day when they flourished, the rulers of realms or principalities, large or small, almost anywhere in the land. Ideally he had everything, wealth and ease and power; no desire was unfulfilled, no pleasure withheld, no purpose thwarted, not knowing what frustration might mean—such is the picture, as impossible as

[18] Quoted in Urquhart, op. cit., p. 64, followed by others in about the same vein.

it is in reality. But what would lead such a creature to do anything! He already had everything—he could not have even the motive to bring any new thing to pass. The only reason why he should act at all is Lila. Just out of sheer sportiveness, with no serious intent, he might do this or that without much more meaning than a baby waving its arms or kicking aimlessly in its cradle. A sorry explanation, to be sure, with neither rhyme nor reason, and yet the one to which the Indian thinker is driven when he attempts to assign a reason for the universe and all it contains.

There remains for us one further consideration: What does such an interpretation of human life, lived under the conditions which this world necessitates, do to our estimate of the worth and dignity of personality and its task and of the significance of human society with its relations and problems? Not only are all these unreal and evanescent, but they can scarcely be taken seriously when they are not the outcome of the deliberate acts of a Being who planned his creation and, when he looked upon what he had made, called it good. As it is, we are introduced to a universe which more or less just happened to come into what existence it has and whose problems are not real but a mirage which is bound to be dissipated in the end. Of course an exception must be made in the case of man in the essence of his being, his real Self, his soul, which is identical with Brahman. I shall hope to do justice to this reality—for it is such—in the subsequent discussion. What is being insisted upon here is that man as we know him and as he knows himself as a thinking, feeling, and willing personality is quite different from his essential Self, which is Brahman. His personality, that which he is as a human being among his fellows, is not a part of the essential Self. This can only mean that man as he experiences himself is not a permanent entity which is to be fitted by discipline for a task and which involves the development of character and the service of mankind. The problems we face are as unreal and unimportant as anything else in the kind of universe the Vedanta proclaims.

Be it said, however, to the lasting credit of many intelligent and high-minded Hindus of today that the implications which have—we think justifiably—been pointed out in the Vedantic scheme of things are not governing their conduct. They are serious-minded lovers of humankind and have set themselves to right the wrongs which are to be found in their country. They are also ardent patriots and have determined to make their land a great and worthy member of the family of nations. They know full well the weaknesses which they must meet and are not daunted by the colossal obstacles which must be overcome. It is not the purpose here to outline their plan of campaign, nor to list the items in the reforms which must be carried through. What is in mind here is to ask what there is in the Vedanta system on which they can lean when they come to the places where the going is hard and they need the help which religion and philosophy should furnish.

Unfortunately what we find would seem to be meager and unfitted for the task. Devanandan declares, "The doctrine of Maya may not necessarily mean that the world is an 'illusion.' But it is obvious that the nearer it approaches such an assertion, the more devitalizing is its effect upon activity and, therefore, upon progress." [19] The air in India is today charged with the ideals of social service and human uplift. The condition of the untouchables must be drastically changed; corruption must be overcome in government service; the status of women must be lifted; illiteracy and poverty must be done away with; land

[19] Op. cit., pp. 218-19. Used by permission of Lutterworth Press.

reform must be carried through—so runs the count, and the list is not exhausted by this brief enumeration. And underneath the outward results which are to be accomplished is the far deeper need to recognize the dignity of human nature, the value of human personality, the demand that man as man be accorded the place of pre-eminence in all that is to be done. But how can such a result be attained when the fundamental conception in their outlook is the unreality of the world and of the human beings who inhabit it? Morality and ethics are not of supreme value and have nothing to do with the state to which men and women are directed as their ultimate objective. Sarma and other Indian writers are glad to acknowledge the example in all forms of betterment furnished during the last century and a half by the Christian missionary. Much of what has been done by Hindus has followed in the trail of the uplift efforts which have been brought in from abroad. The schoolteacher, the doctor and the nurse, the agricultural expert, and others have set the pattern. Indians not only have emulated these philanthropically minded men and women but have exceeded them in many cases by the extent of their far-flung campaign to ameliorate the condition of those in need of these ministrations. Notable in this respect has been the service rendered by the Ramakrishna Mission—but of course it has not been confined to that organization.

But can this endeavor continue to find sufficient guidance and inspiration to support the weight of an undertaking not only of decades but of centuries? Swami Vivekananda thought that the Vedanta as taught by Shankara was all that was needed, as do the leaders who follow in his train. A little reinterpretation here and there is all that is necessary; the basic principles are there and are sufficient. But again we hear Devanandan calling our attention to the fact that "every aspect of Hindu life is affected in an unprecedented way by the acceptance in practice of alien principles of conduct and life-outlook which are subversive of the basic assumptions of the religious theory on which Hindu India's thought-fabric is built." Nothing permanent can be built except on the deep conviction of the supreme value of man as man. "This is strange doctrine to Hinduism. . . . The idea of personality, as we now conceive it, is the outcome of the modern science of psychology, inspired largely by the Christian doctrines of God and man." [20] Only a theistic belief would seem to be sufficient to bear the burden of enthusiasm and hope necessary for lifting life up to new levels. We find Radhakrishnan somewhat elusive at this point. As a Vedantist and yet a profound interpreter of present-day trends in India, he believes he can find in the *Upanishads* and in the *Gita* all that is needed to undergird the passion of his altruistic fellow countrymen for the remaking of their nation and its social life. I am not alone in my impression that ideas alien and incongruous with the real meaning of these ancient writings are being read into them from sources quite foreign to their spirit. When Radhakrishnan uses the word "God," it is at times difficult to determine whether he is referring to the theistic conception of the Creator God of the Christian tradition or the monistic conception as held by Shankara and his followers—and it makes a real difference which is meant. When he uses the term "kingdom of God" to describe the blessedness of a future day, one wonders where in the Vedanta he can find anything commensurate with the idea as used by Jesus Christ. Is it not a Hinduism very unlike the Hinduism of the Indian classics which Radhakrishnan is unfolding and defending in his writings? We can only be deeply satisfied that he is holding such views; our con-

[20] *Ibid.*, pp. 221, 223.

cern is that the day may come when those who have been given to understand that Hinduism possesses in its own tradition all that is necessary to give meaning to their endeavors and furnish the motivation and power to do what is required will be disillusioned. Will they not realize that they are deeply in need of a message which comes as a gospel, good tidings of what God can and will do in Christ to those who have caught the vision of a new life for themselves and their beloved India? Can we avoid the conclusion that in the end Indians must make a choice and come to a decision between the Vedanta conception and that which is contained in the gospel of Christ?

Chapter Five

The Nature of Man and His Status

VEDANTA teaches "that man's real nature is divine. If, in this universe, there is an underlying Reality, a Godhead, then that Godhead must be omnipresent. If the Godhead is omnipresent, It must be within each one of us and within every creature and object. Therefore man, in his true nature, is God." Thus we read in *Vedanta in America*, an official leaflet of the Ramakrishna Mission. So man is essentially divine; he is God. On the other hand, what is his actual status among his fellows? This is determined by his position in the caste system, which in turn has been an essential feature of Hinduism.

This doctrine of man's divinity is an accepted doctrine among the intelligentsia in India. The treasurer of the state of Madhya Pradesh in the course of an address before the Leonard Theological College, a union Christian institution, declared, "You are divine," and emphasized his point by repeating, "We are all divine." He said he was a follower of Sri Aurobindo, who was at that time (1950) still living. We may use words from the pen of Sri Aurobindo to illustrate the widespread conviction of the divinity of man: "But ultimately man himself comes to realize that the Supreme Reality and the true inner self of his being are one, that the soul is the very seed of the Divine, and the All-Supreme is in fact the Self." [1] These statements, and a hundred others like them, do not mean that men may

[1] Quoted in Nathaniel Pearson, *Sri Aurobindo and the Soul Quest of Man*, pp. 55-56.

94

become divine but that they are divine now, that they can never become more divine than they are in their present condition, even though they may not recognize the fact and as little as they may seem to be divine in their conduct and attitudes.

How does the Christian attitude differ from this? In the first place and most significantly, man is a creature, not self-existent or eternal but created by God and dependent on him for everything he is and has, including life itself. God not only is responsible for the origin of man but is the "determiner of his destiny," to use the phrase of James Bissett Pratt. So man is not divine; he does not share the power and prerogatives of God. Man is always the recipient; God is the giver and sustainer of all that man is and has. This means that there is a qualitative difference between God and man, one that can never be changed.

But on the other hand, we are told that God created man "in his own image." "So God created man in his own image," are the words in the Genesis account, or as Moffatt puts it, "So God formed man in his own likeness" (1:27). What do "image" and "likeness" mean? Let S. R. Driver in his commentary on Genesis lead us in our interpretation:

It is (1) something which evidently forms the ground and basis of his entire preeminence above animals; (2) it is something which is transmitted to his descendants, and belongs therefore to man in general, and not solely to man in a state of primitive innocence; (3) it relates, from the nature of the case, to man's immaterial nature. It can be nothing but the gift of *self-conscious reason*, which is possessed by man, but by no other animal.[2]

Other commentators are not so sure about what the Genesis account involves, but all are agreed that man is distinguished

[2] *The Book of Genesis*, 9th ed., p. 15.

from the animals as a being who can enter into personal relations with God.

When the Hebrew psalmist looked at man in his smallness as contrasted with the celestial world in its grandeur and expanse, he exclaimed,

> When I look at thy heavens, the work of thy fingers,
>   the moon and the stars which thou hast established;
> what is man that thou art mindful of him,
>   and the son of man that thou dost care for him?

But he looks deeper and realizes that this puny creature has what no other part of the creation possesses:

> Yet thou hast made him little less than God,
>   and dost crown him with glory and honor.
> Thou hast given him dominion over the works of thy hands;
>   thou hast put all things under his feet.

The whole purpose of the psalm, however, is not so much to evelate man as to glorify God, who has done all these wonderful things:

> O Lord, our Lord,
>   how majestic is thy name in all the earth!
>   (Ps. 8:3-4, 5-6, 9 R.S.V.)

This is one side of the shield; but on the other side man is not divine, not only because of his dependence on God for creation and preservation but because he has sinned and come far "short of the glory of God." He has deliberately run counter to the will of his Maker and incurred the divine displeasure by his pride and self-assertion. This has debased his life and corrupted his nature and all his relations with his fellow men. He has estranged himself from God and is at enmity with him and his will. In the words of Alan Richardson, "The Bible consistently teaches the paradoxical character of human nature. On the one hand, man is 'but a little lower than God.' . . . On the other hand, man is 'like unto the beasts that perish' (Ps. 49:12, 20; cf. Ps. 144:3 f.); his mortality is the outward and visible sign of the inner corruption of his nature." [3] The Vedanta is exceedingly hesitant to use the word "sin" with its implication of alienation from God. "The Vedantists prefer the word 'obstacle' to the word 'sin' because, if we think of ourselves as sinners and miserable, we forget the Godhead within us and lapse into that mood of doubt, despondency, and weakness which is the greatest obstacle of all." [4] We shall discover that this failure to acknowledge the true nature of sin and its entail in suffering and deterioration reduces the possibility of penitence and forgiveness practically to nonexistence in the Vedanta and other systems which have the same conception of sin.

There are those who consider themselves within the Christian ranks who, upon being asked if they believe in the divinity of Christ, have a ready answer, "Yes, we believe Christ was divine, but so are we," the difference being one of degree and not of kind. The matter is referred to here because of the ease with which this position slides over into and becomes almost, if not completely, identical with that of the Vedantist and his claim that man is inherently divine. It is not the purpose here to present the evidence for the divinity of Christ, but on the basis of belief in his divinity to show the incongruity of the assertion that man is divine, as is Christ, though to a lesser degree. The scriptural evidence places Christ on the creative, Godward side in the universe and man on the human side as the

[3] *Theological Word Book of the Bible*, art. "Adam, Man."
[4] *Vedanta in America*. Used by permission of the Vedanta Society of Southern California.

recipient of God's favors in Christ. He is weak and sinful and powerless to rise in his own strength to the position where he can have communion and fellowship with God. In the prologue of John's Gospel we are told, "But to all who received him [Christ], who believed in his name, he gave power to become children of God" (1:12 R.S.V.). The word "power" might be rendered "right" or "authority." As the creation of God mankind is related to God; they are his sons, partaking of his "image," but sin has alienated men so that it is necessary that a gift, a priceless boon, be conferred upon them that they may come into possession of the "right," the privilege of becoming in a peculiar sense the "children of God." Christ is divine as we are not; he is the one who in the mercy of God confers upon us the possibility of being reconciled to God and living in joy and fellowship with him.

While in Hinduism man is essentially divine, this does not mean that man in his present condition is perfect or beautiful in character, as a truly divine being should be. Hinduism is realistic in its attitude toward man and recognizes that men are not living the lives they should. An elaborate ethical system with rules and regulations indicates that man is taken as he is and must give himself to moral discipline to overcome his weaknesses and develop a noble character. The Laws of Manu are one of the great repositories of the ancient ethical system. Every aspect of human life and its relations is given detailed direction. The laws are codified in twenty-nine sections in which the duties of individuals and of society, of rulers and heads of households, civil and criminal law, the conduct of family life, what foods are lawful and what forbidden, and many other items are laid upon the heart and conscience of the people. There are also the Grihya, Dharma, and Srauta Sutras, going even further than the Laws of Manu in describing the obligation resting upon the people. This is not the place to enter upon a discussion of the nature of these regulations; I mention them to show that while man may be considered essentially divine, he is far from perfect and is in need of training, direction, and discipline.

All this sounds very familiar to Western ears and need not be enlarged upon. Hinduism takes man as he is and seeks to mold him into what he ought to be. But this is not all. Take but another step and we of the West find ourselves in a strange land. The double doctrine of transmigration and Karma makes a tremendous difference in the entire ethical outlook of India— in fact, of the whole East—as contrasted with the West. Even in India the doctrine is not a part of the religion which the Aryans brought into the land in the second millennium before our era. It is not to be found in the four *Vedas* and only begins to make its appearance in the legalistic *Brahmanas* attached to the Vedic texts. We must wait until the appearance of the *Upanishads*, that is, about 500 B.C., to find the doctrine full-blown and powerful in the religious theories of the seers and thinkers of the Hinduism which was taking the form from which it has never departed.

The acute thinkers among the Brahmin[5] priests and those responsible for the *Upanishads* took a doctrine which was crude and unfinished and elaborated it into the mighty doctrine of transmigration and Karma as it has come down through the centuries. We cannot overestimate its significance in Hindu religion. Listen to the late Govinda Das, of the Benares Hindu University, in his *Hinduism*:

This law of Karma . . . is the Key-stone of the arch over which has been built up, through the course of ages, the vast edifice of Hinduism. Knock this out and the splendid structure crumbles to

[5] Spelled "Brahmin" to distinguish the name of a caste from "Brahman," the Absolute.

THE INEVITABLE CHOICE

the ground. It is no wonder that we so strenuously pin our faith to it, and defend this vital position against all attacks. We are prepared under the various modern stresses—economic, social, etc., to loosen our hold on many another practice and belief regarded as fundamental in the earlier days, but not on this.[6]

No further testimonies are needed to place this doctrine in the high place which it occupies in Hindu thinking.

What is this doctrine which has been so determinative in the past and so potent at the present day? We may take the simple statement of Govinda Das as giving the gist of the doctrine, "As a man sows so he reaps," [7] or a fuller and very early statement in the *Chandogya Upanishad* (v. 10.7), "Those whose conduct has been pleasing, will quickly attain a pleasing birth, ... but those whose conduct has been abominable, will quickly attain an abominable birth, the birth of a dog, or a hog, or an outcaste." It is given somewhat differently by M. Hiriyanna: "The doctrine extends the principle of causation to the sphere of human conduct and teaches that, as every event in the physical world is determined by its antecedents, so everything that happens in the moral realm is preordained." [8] In other words, what a man finds himself to be now is the result of previous actions, and what he is to become is determined by what he does now plus what he has done in the past. One more statement on this point, coming from Swami Vivekananda, the founder of the Ramakrishna Mission, may be quoted:

Any word, any action, any thought that produces an effect is called Karma. Thus the law of Karma means the law of causation, of inevitable cause and effect. Whatever we see or feel or do, whatever action there is anywhere in the universe, while being the

[6] P. 217.
[7] *Ibid.*
[8] *The Essentials of Indian Philosophy*, p. 46. Used by permission of George Allen & Unwin, Ltd. and The Macmillan Co.

effect of past work on the one hand, becomes, on the other, a cause in its turn and produces its own effect. Each one of us is the effect of an infinite past. The child is ushered into the world not as something flashing from the hands of nature, as poets delight so much to depict, but he has the burden of an infinite past; for good or evil he comes to work out his own past deeds. This makes the differentiation. This is the law of Karma. Each one of us is the maker of his own fate.[9]

"Why do bad people flourish and good people suffer?" asks Govinda Das. His answer is, "The bad man who flourished had a stock of good Karma yet unexhausted to his credit, while the sufferings of the good man were due to some as yet unexhausted evil Karma." [10] So a separation must be made between the *tendencies* which a man inherits from himself in a former life which determine his actions in this life, and the *results* in suffering or prosperity which a man finds to be his lot in this life because of deeds done in some former life. These results he cannot change by an iota; they must be endured or enjoyed as the case may be to the last ounce of requital or reward, suffering or enjoyment. Of course the whole thing works automatically. How can all this result in anything but inertia and supine submission and acceptance? There must be some way to meet a situation like this, and it is provided by the "ways" of salvation which we have yet to consider. But nothing can release a man from bearing the full effect of an evil deed except the one "way" which leads to final and complete emancipation, that is, in the loss of his own individuality in his eventual absorption in the attributeless Brahman, an experience which is extolled as the quintessence of bliss.

This teaching, as has already been suggested, is a double doc-

[9] Swami Nikhilananda, Vivekananda: A Biography, pp. 199-200. Used by permission.
[10] Op. cit., p. 216.

trine, transmigration-Karma, which while always found in combination, may be considered in its two aspects. In the first place there is transmigration, or rebirth of souls.[11] Hinduism has always posited the existence of the soul, called atman. The soul is imperishable and persists from one life to another through the eternities. "Since each life is the requital of foregoing action, and since the actions of each new life demand another for their reward or punishment, the process of birth and death, samsara, can have had no beginning, and can have no end." [12] "No beginning," "no end"—that is a startling thing to declare. A statement by a Hindu scholar, R. N. Dandekar, deals with the question very pertinently:

If each existence is the result of the actions in the previous existence, then how could there be a first birth in the series of rebirths? Such a question is philosophically inadmissible, according to Hindu thought, for the world of existence is beginningless. It is impossible to visualize an individual without antecedents. If the essential self were unaffected by any antecedents, it would not be born at all and thus would not assume individuality.[13]

So every man is fated to an endless succession of lives in which his soul shall be compelled to live under conditions determined entirely by his conduct in former lives—in health or illness, happiness or discomfort, wealth or poverty, in high caste or low or in between, happily married or mated with a shrew, with obedient children or bad, and so on through all the

[11] We should distinguish between "transmigration" and "rebirth." Both terms are used in Hinduism, for Hindus believe in a soul which transmigrates or is reborn, but "transmigration" is not used in Buddhism, for the Buddha taught that there was no soul to migrate to another body in another life. See Ward, op. cit., I, ch. x, Hinayana, 83 ff.

[12] J. N. Farquhar, An Outline of the Religious Literature of India, p. 35.

[13] Morgan, Kenneth W. (Editor). The Religion of the Hindus, art. "The Role of Man in Hinduism," p. 129. Copyright 1953 The Ronald Press Company.

vicissitudes of life. The inevitability of this uncertain succession of lives became an increasingly unbearable burden. The Hindu has lived in a state of dread as he peered into the unknown and precarious future, where there was no hope of a change from this uncertainty.

We have yet to consider the three "ways" of salvation, or release, which developed in the early history of Hinduism. Just here, however, we may ask: "Salvation" or "release" from what? And the significant answer is, release from the necessity of being born again times without number. The Hindu dreads the necessity of rebirth to the extent that salvation from this necessity is looked upon as the greatest boon which he can imagine. This helps us to realize that Hinduism is a pessimistic religion, that is, from the standpoint of the worth of human life lived under human conditions on this earth. There is no appeal. Karma is not a law or force under the control of a beneficent deity, or any deity in fact, even Brahman; it is an impersonal power which goes its relentless way with no counterforce to stop or control it. No wonder a kind of apathy takes possession of the life of the Hindu, discouraging endeavor and not allowing hope to have its uplifting place in his life.

Hindu thinkers of today are well aware of certain intellectual problems which arise when the law of Karma is brought into contact with modern thought. One of these is the charge that Karma is deterministic and takes away the freedom which a man ought to have to be a complete personality. There is unanimity among thinking Hindus at the present time that freedom is a necessary attribute of human personality. One does not have to read many pages in *The Philosophy of Sarvepalli Radhakrishnan* to know that that eminent Indian philosopher is a passionate believer in human freedom. He declares, "The cards in the game of life are given to us. . . . But we can

103

call as we please, lead what suit we will, and as we play, we gain
or lose. And there is freedom." [14] But he does not face the problem as directly as M. Hiriyanna, who says, "As every event in the
physical world is determined by its antecedents, so everything
that happens in the moral realm is preordained. If all that man
does is preordained, it may be asked whether the doctrine does
not become fatalistic and therefore leave no room for the exer-
cise of freedom." After a brief discussion of the meaning of
freedom Hiriyanna comes to this explanation:

> The present conduct of a person and the good or evil that follows
> from it are *due to his own actions* done in one state of existence,
> if not in another. Destiny thus becomes only another name for deeds
> done in previous births. There being therefore no external Fate
> constraining man to act as he does . . . the doctrine does not there-
> fore lead to fatalism.[15]

This candid statement demands careful scrutiny. Hiriyanna's
argument rests on the assumption—and it is truly an assumption—that the person now living and acting is the identical
person who performed acts in a previous existence which determine what he now thinks and does. But supposing that for
the sake of the argument we admit that we are dealing with the
same person in different lives or rebirths, are we convinced that
the man now living has true freedom? To which we may reply:
Would it be possible to imagine anything more external to a
person now living than a supposed person whom he never
knew, whose acts he cannot remember, whose whereabouts and
environment and character are completely unknown to him?
According to Hiriyanna a man's life and character are made
what they are by an influence of which he is totally ignorant

[14] *The Hindu View of Life*, p. 75.
[15] *Op. cit.*, pp. 46-47. (Italics are mine.)

104

and which must of necessity remain a complete blank to him. Is it not as deadening to be thus determined as to be under the compulsion of an inexorable fate, or a deity, or any other force from which there is no escape?

Hiriyanna goes further and seeks to show that the Karma doctrine is based on high ethical principles, so "that there is absolute justice in the rewards and punishments that fall to our lot in life. . . . The law of Karma accordingly is not a blind mechanical law, but is essentially ethical." [16] How can there be any assurance that the doctrine is based on moral principles when Karma is a blind, impersonal force not under the control of a power or a deity of ethical concern? Blind, uncontrolled force does not give backing to a belief in the presence of moral distinctions in acts or results. And yet the claim is made that the "Karma doctrine is grounded in the moral view of the universe," [17] and therefore the rewards and punishments constitute a discipline of natural consequences to educate a man morally. "The moral view of the universe"—this shows how earnestly Hiriyanna desires to moralize the law of Karma; but let us face the situation in which a man finds himself in the midst of the varying situations in life, good and bad. How can a man be educated morally by what comes to him in life when he cannot know what he did in a former life which brought the evil which he now suffers? Moral education must be built on knowledge, knowledge of the cause of his suffering in the act which is bringing the present evil result; then only can he intelligently start out in another direction and mend his ways and not be guilty of the same evil deed or attitude again. How deeply is morality embedded in this universe of ours when Brahman, the Absolute, is beyond the distinction between right and wrong?

[16] *Ibid.*, p. 48.
[17] *Ibid.*, p. 49.

Morality can scarcely be of supreme value in the universe where the only true reality, Brahman, has no concern with right or wrong. As A. G. Hogg so pertinently suggests, sanctity and holiness in this life are not the Hindu ideal; the Hindu longs rather for serenity. He puts it thus: Christ "finds the Indian sheep tangled in a helpless longing for serenity rather than sanctity, oppressed by enchainment to the 'wheel' of birth and rebirth rather than by terrors of a guilty conscience." [18] May this not be the reason why deities in the Hindu pantheon today have lived lives and performed deeds according to the accepted mythology which no decent man could condone and which cannot be taken as an example for a noble-minded man to follow? Does not the old aphorism "Like gods, like people" have relevancy here? It is a question for serious-minded Hindus to take to heart and ponder deeply.

Hogg also calls attention to the fact that the law of Karma is purely individualistic. It has no place for the social effect of wrongdoing, when the well-known fact is that the evil deeds of a man reach out beyond himself and affect others, in some case many others. It is also true that the good deeds of a man may bring blessing to others, not only in his time but for many years after. To adhere to the law of Karma, that all the good or evil a man may now be enjoying or suffering is due to his own acts in a former existence, is flying in the face of the evidence of facts. What Hitler did plunged hundreds of thousands of men, women, and children into a condition of desperate need and suffering, people as innocent of Hitler's evil deeds and as undeserving of the fate which overtook them as the people in America or India, who suffered little or nothing. On the other hand we can think of many benefactors of the race through

[18] *The Christian Message to the Hindu*, pp. 92, 95.

whose deeds many have been blessed who have not deserved
the benefits which have come to them any more than the
thousands to whom these benefits have been denied. The supreme example, of course, which comes at once to the mind of
the followers of Christ is that through his undeserved suffering
and death untold benefits have come to millions of men and
women who have lived since the day of the supreme sacrifice
on Calvary. When we find ourselves in this realm, we quickly
discover that the law of Karma ceases to be of any assistance in
the attempt to account for the conditions in which people find
themselves. Human life is social as well as individual. Living
our lives in a fellowship, as we all must do, makes it inescapable
that what one does affects others and is responsible for results
not only in his generation but often in generations yet to be
born.

Hindu writers declare that according to the law of Karma a
man inherits from himself in former births not only the penalty
for evil deeds but certain tendencies to action which determine
how he will act from time to time.[19] This would seem to
strengthen the hold of Karma on a man and his acts, for is he
not in a very real sense foreordained by these tendencies to act
in accordance with them? But the Hindu of today with his
sincere belief in freedom will not have it that way. We may let
Sarma speak: "We should not exaggerate the operations of the
Law of Karma, but should always remember that the law can
be controlled and even overcome by a properly trained will,
especially when that will is made subservient to a higher will
than ours." [20] As one continues, however, to read and think
about this doctrine of Karma, the conviction grows that there
is a fundamental inconsistency between Karma and freedom;

[19] Hiriyanna, *op. cit.*, p. 49.
[20] *Op. cit.*, p. 156.

the two simply do not go together. It would seem that just so far as a Hindu thinker goes in his affirmation of freedom, he is to that extent denying the operation of the law of Karma. He cannot have it both ways; the two are incompatible, and if by definition or explanation he attempts to show that freedom has a place in the scheme of things in which Karma also prevails, he is running counter to the law of Karma as it has been interpreted from ancient times.

In considering the operation of the law of Karma, we can proceed only a very short distance before we find that one of the most important points at which Karma impinges on the life of a Hindu is caste and the caste system. He is a member of the caste to which he belongs by being born into it—he cannot join a caste; he is a birthright member or not a member at all.[21] If he belongs to the Brahmin or some other high-caste family, it is because that is where he belongs according to the law of Karma; and if he finds himself in a caste down at the lower rungs of the social ladder or even a despised Untouchable, it is for the same reason—he is where he is because of acts in previous lives. So here is a kind of indicator, an outward sign of what a man has been like in his moral conduct somewhere back in his former experience. This makes it necessary in studying man in the Hindu system to know something about the meaning of caste in actual life.

In the first place, there is nothing exactly like the Hindu caste system in any other country or society in the world. The Western world does have class distinctions, some of which are inevitable and some most reprehensible. There are the intelligentsia as contrasted with the uneducated and even the illiterate. Do what one may, it is impossible to deny the great gulf which

[21] Today caste and caste laws are changing. Intercaste marriages do occur. The old rigidity is giving way to the demands of modern life.

separates people on the basis of intellectual achievement and not to realize that this does separate people in their work and social relations. On the other hand, there are the contemptible pride and presumption of the wealthy, especially the newly rich, who quickly come to feel their superiority over the poor and the underprivileged and show it in their conduct. It is possible to list other forms of class cleavage, one of the worst of which is the feeling of superiority, yes, inherent superiority, of white people in their relations with the Negroes in the Western world and nonwhites everywhere. And yet when all has been said which might be said about these and other divisions in Western society and in countries in the East outside the Hindu community, it remains true that the caste system in India is sui generis.[22]

One clue to the origin of caste is found in the Sanskrit word for caste, varna, which means "color." It will be remembered that the Aryans were white men coming into India from the northwest and that they came into contact with the dark-skinned Dravidians, the "Southerners." It seems impossible to avoid the conclusion that caste had at least as one of its causes the attempt of the Aryans to preserve the whiteness of their skin and the purity of their blood by having little or nothing to do with the "natives" of dark skin. The attempt failed completely—no one in Hinduism now makes anything of racial differences in determining caste distinctions. The tendency today in the attempt to explain caste is to lay much greater stress upon occupational differences, such as we find in the original distinctions in the last book of the Rig-Veda. But with all the many attempts to give a more or less complete account of the

[22] For discussion of caste as uniquely Hindu see J. H. Hutton, Caste in India, pp. 40-41, pp. 116 ff., an authoritative volume by the professor of social anthropology in the University of Cambridge.

origins of caste, no satisfying explanation has been found. What we realize is that the system exists and forms a most important religious and social factor in the life of Hindus.

It is far more important to learn the effect of the caste system upon men and women in their individual lives, their status as members of the community, and their relations with one another than to be able to determine its origins and its development. The *Laws of Manu*,[23] 4th or 5th century A.D., is a "law book claiming the allegiance of all Aryans and generally acknowledged by them." [24] The evident purpose of these laws is to exalt the Brahmin to the place of supreme authority and sanctity and to subordinate all others to him, especially the menial Sudras. The Brahmin "is by right the lord of this whole creation." [25] "By his origin alone a Brahmana [Brahmin] is a deity even for the gods, and (his teaching is) authoritative for men." [26] At the other extreme is the Sudra. "One occupation only the lord presented to the Sudra, to serve meekly even these (other) three castes." [27] "A Sudra . . . shall be excluded . . . from all the duties and rights of an Aryan." [28] He was probably one of the Dravidians, the dark-skinned people already in the land when the Aryans arrived. He is very low in the human scale. The same penance is exacted for the killing of a "cat, an ichneumon, a bluejay, a frog, a dog, an iguana, an owl, or a crow" as for the murder of a Sudra.[29] With what may be said of the miserable condition of the Sudra, we must pity the Brahmin as well. As Mrs. Sinclair Stevenson puts it: "How is

[23] Buhler, op. cit., Vol. XXV.
[24] *Ibid.*, p. xlv. Used by permission of Oxford University Press.
[25] *Ibid.*, I, 93.
[26] *Ibid.*, XI, 85.
[27] *Ibid.*, I, 91.
[28] *Ibid.*, II, 103.
[29] *Ibid.*, XI, 132.

a man to overcome selfishness when his own sacred law teaches him that 'No collection of wealth must be made by a Sudra, even though he be able (to do it); for a Sudra who has acquired wealth gives pain to the Brahmans?' " [30]

During the centuries the people who have inherited the ignominy of the Sudra of the early days are the outcastes, the Untouchables, the "exterior castes," to use several of the names by which they are known. "The number of these exterior castes in India was found at the census of 1931 to be more than 50 millions, or 21% of a Hindu population of 239 odd millions." [31] Hutton quotes from J. Wilson, *Indian Caste*, who gives a long list of the regulations which govern and for the most part restrict and hamper the lives of Untouchables, and closes with these words, "It interferes, in short, with all the relations and events of life, and with what precedes and follows . . . life." [32] No system in the world has ever been devised so well calculated to shatter self-respect and reduce life to a shameful subservience as the caste system. So utterly contemned are these miserable outcastes, so contaminating is contact with them, that a Brahmin will throw away the food he is about to eat if the shadow of an Untouchable should fall on it. Other serious counts are being made against the whole system by Hindus as well as outsiders, but it is at the point of the attitude toward and treatment of the Untouchables that opinion is being centered in the minds of thoughtful Hindus at the present time.

A long list could be made of those notable Indians who have taken a stand against Untouchability. Here, as at other points, Mohandas Gandhi comes into the picture. He recognized how terrible was the plight of these fifty or more millions of his

[30] *The Rites of the Twice-Born*, p. 442. Used by permission of Oxford University Press.
[31] Hutton, *op. cit.*, p. 113.
[32] *Ibid.*, p. 79.

fellow Indians and set himself to raise their status. Instead of thinking of them as outcastes and Untouchables, he gave them a new name, Harijan, or the "Children of God," the deity being Hari, one of the names of Vishnu. He upset all the conventions and adopted into his family a little outcaste girl. As a result of what he and many others were doing, untouchability was outlawed in the new Indian constitution. We read in the leading article in *The Statesman*, New Delhi, December 1, 1948, that "without opposition the Constituent Assembly this morning [November 29] accepted an Article in the Draft Constitution providing for the abolition of untouchability and making the enforcement of this disability punishable by law," and this is now a part of the basic law of the land. Of considerable significance is the fact that the leading spirit in the writing of the constitution was B. R. Ambedkar, who thereby earned the right to the title of Father of the Indian Constitution. And Ambedkar, at that time Law Member of Nehru's Cabinet, is an Untouchable himself, thus giving the lie to the opinion, widely held in the India of the past, that the Untouchables had no souls, that they were on the level of the beasts of the field. Nothing could be expected of them no matter how much should be given to them of opportunity for development. Strict Hindus have been very chary in recognizing the manner in which Christian missionaries have lifted hundreds and even thousands of these despised people to a place of honor and respectability to become worthy members of the communities in which they reside.

Now that untouchability has been outlawed by the National Legislative Assembly as well as by the governments of several of the Indian states, young Indian patriots have frequently asserted that the battle has been won and that they can tell audiences and individuals in America and elsewhere that untouchability no longer exists. We need constantly to be reminded that the enactment of a provision in the constitution or a law by a legislative body means far less in India than in a Western country. The Indian village—and the real India consists of 500,000 to 600,000 villages—is to a great extent a law-to itself, where the old customs prevail and old prejudices are only beginning to give way to enlightened public opinion. The old caste restrictions still hold, and caste regulations are still the rules which are followed. In time—how long, no one can tell—the change so much needed will come; but that day is only beginning in most of India. The situation in the cities and certain industrial centers is different. Here men and women are thrown together and have so many contacts that mingling among castes, especially the upper-caste men, is frequent; and announcements are not infrequent of marriages which cross caste boundaries. But even in the cities the recognition of the rights of the Untouchables is exceedingly slow.

One of the most important questions before thinking Indians today is how far it is wise to go in changing the system. Many realize that something must be done. How is it possible to build up a unified India with a common patriotism in which all may participate when the highest loyalty for ages has been to one's caste? How can India possibly meet the requirements of a democracy which can be built up only on the foundation of the recognition of the equal rights of all? Many do not recognize that a true democracy can come only out of a deeper belief in the brotherhood of man based on the common fatherhood of God. They do accept the fact, however, that a change must come over the attitudes of men and women as they think of their fellows who are under such great disabilities. All these men stand for the abolition of untouchability. This is one of the planks in the platform of the Ramakrishna Mission. But

113

even when agreement has been reached with reference to untouchability, what of the division of the people into the four original castes of the *Rig-Veda*, which have been mentioned? Many hold even today that they are of divine origin and should continue to bind them forever. This is true of Radhakrishnan as well as of Gandhi, the former going so far as to praise the caste system in Indian history as having proved to be a beneficial provision. He is opposed, however, by a number of very enlightened persons who believe that the caste system has always been a hindrance to Indian progress, that there is and has always been something unjust and unfair about it. Not often, however, do we find an Indian who will go as far as to declare that the only hope for the future of their beloved country is to abolish not only untouchability but the whole caste system. Having discussed two attitudes, that of the retention of the entire system as divine and that of holding fast to the four original divisions, R. N. Dandekar proceeds:

The third attitude toward caste today is that of the social reformers who advocate a complete extermination of castes by all possible means. . . . It is rightly pointed out that the gravest evil of the caste system is that it has rendered Indian society undemocratic and a sociological myth. One, therefore, feels inclined strongly to support the plea that an active nationwide campaign be launched against caste, both through governmental and private agencies.[33]

What Dandekar senses is that any society divided into watertight compartments on the basis of birth and birth alone denies the fundamental principles of democracy. Such a system runs counter to the fundamental principles that "all men are created free and equal," and without that a society is bound to deny fundamental rights to men who are thwarted by being born

[33] Morgan, *op. cit.*, p. 150.

in one caste and not in another—unable to change their status.

Indian Christians are alive to this need. R. D. Immanuel deals with the problems very cogently in his volume *The Influence of Hinduism on Indian Christians*. He states that "the Indians' longing is for an ideal society in which each will realize his best . . . besides ministering to his eternal or spiritual needs." It must provide "(a) social anchorage; (b) tangible higher value which he can serve; (c) a fairly reliable protection from the harsh assaults on him by the cruel economic, social, and political forces; and (d) a guide and refuge in times of personal afflictions and distresses," and finally "the Church must be to him a coordinating factor of all the aspects of life." [34] This sounds very much like the ideal cherished by Christians of what their churches should be in America and the West, but with the difference that in India the young convert is often cast off by his old friends and relations and must have a new fellowship which will fulfill all the needs and earnest desires of one who has given himself to Christ and must look to his new friends for everything.

"For just as the body is one and has many members, and all members of the body, though many, are one body, so it is with Christ. For by one Spirit we were all baptized into one body— Jews or Greeks, slaves or free—and all were made to drink of one spirit." (I Cor. 12:12-13 R.S.V.) Instead of "Jews or Greeks, slaves or free," we might justifiably read, "Indians and Americans, low caste or Brahmins"—we are one in Christ— that is the Christian offer to the caste man in Hinduism.

[34] Pp. 32-33.

Chapter Six

Salvation and Final Destiny

SALVATION in Hinduism is radically different from salvation in Christianity. In our religion to be saved means release from the burden and guilt of sin, here and hereafter, entering a new life of victory over one's lower nature, and fellowship with God in the community of the saved. It is the restoration of a broken relationship, broken by sin. In Hinduism, on the other hand, salvation has as its aim escape from the effects of the law of Karma. When a man has realized the goal of his longing, he will never be reborn again. The law of Karma simply ceases to operate in his case, but unfortunately this is not the outlook for almost all the human race in the seeable future. All except a few in the present world look forward to no more than a possible mitigation of their present condition in a happier lot in their next birth, as a result of meritorious deeds in this or in former lives. The disparity between the two religions in respect of final destiny is equally great, if not greater. It is the difference between continuous, conscious fellowship in heaven with God in the company of the redeemed and in Hinduism absorption in the attributeless Brahman, the Absolute, in a state which has no likeness to what we know as consciousness, activity, or loving fellowship.

We may take the occasion here, as at a number of other places, to stand still and wonder at the philosophical acumen of the Indian people. More than any other people in the history of the world, with the possible exception of the Greeks, the

Indian has shown the power of thinking through the most difficult questions and finding a solution. The solution may not be
to our liking—it frequently was not satisfactory even to Indians
themselves—but far more than other people the Indian es-
sayed to solve the problem of the meaning of life and destiny.
Not only is this true of the highly educated scholar and thinker;
but as is not the case elsewhere, the man down in the ranks has
been able to enter, at least to a certain extent, into the meaning
of what has been said and written. Why should this be true of
the Indian, not only of Rig-Vedic Aryan, who came in from
the outside, but of the indigenous Dravidian, so different from
the Aryan in origin and development? Has anyone been able to
answer that question? About all that has been done is to note
the fact and wonder at it. It must also be said that the Indian
has not been equally noted as a man of will power. The criticism
has been made that the danger has been to indulge in endless
talk and do little or nothing about it—to the exasperation of
the man of the West who wants to do something whether he
has thought much about its significance or not.

Indian thinking for the most part has been in the realm of
religion. To put it in the words of a very appreciative American
student, "All systems of Hindu Philosophy are in complete
agreement that the purpose of philosophy is the extinction of
sorrow and suffering and that the method is by the acquisition
of knowledge of the true nature of things which aims to free
man from the bondage of ignorance which all teachers agree
is the cause of human suffering." [1] This statement is true of
Indian classical philosophy, in fact, of all the writings of Indian
thinkers until very recent years. But now India has come into
contact with the West. Here in our modern Western world

[1] Theos Bernard, *Hindu Philosophy*, p. 2.

philosophers have looked on their craft and its purpose quite differently. Breaking away from the medieval attachment of philosophy to religion, the modern philosopher looks upon his task as absolutely free from what he would consider the trammels of religion and theology. He seeks to understand the meaning of the universe and human existence by the processes of human reason alone, without dependence on religion or a revelation from on high. He is eager to discover unity in the universe and arrive at coherence in his thinking, so that he may have understanding and satisfaction. He is dealing with subjects very close to religion—how to account for the origin of things, if there be a beginning at all; how to explain the meaning of life, of human life in particular, what the end and purpose of existence. He is not trying to defend religious attitudes and in many cases believes that religion is not essential and has an incorrect interpretation of life and its meaning. On the other hand, there are many philosophers who are deeply religious men, but the distinction is clearly made even here between the conclusions they reach through philosophical reflection and those which have come to them through religious faith and belief.

Within the last half century and particularly the past twenty-five years, the situation in India has begun to change. Contact with the outlook of Western thinkers has to a growing extent made a separation between the purposes of philosophical speculation and that of theological thinking. A survey of *The Indian Philosophical Congress Jubilee Commemoration Volume, 1950,* is very convincing evidence of the change. One of the contributions made to this volume is by Rasvihary Das, lecturer in philosophy, Calcutta University, entitled "Philosophy as an Autonomous Spiritual Activity." Here we read: "Philosophy is thinking and reflective thinking at that, and there can be no thinking in the true sense of the term unless there is complete freedom."

Also, "I believe the time is now ripe, *even in this country*, to declare unequivocally that philosophy exists for itself and does not need to justify itself by any service it may possibly render either to science or to religion." [2] This is a new note in India and means that a great change has come over the thinking of at least some Indian students.

Time has been taken to call attention to this new phenomenon so that it may be seen in contrast to the Vedanta philosophy with which we are particularly concerned. It will be recalled that in speaking of the classical philosophers Shankara, Ramanuja, and Madhva the statement was made that no significant addition to Indian thought had been made since their day. They were distinctively religious philosophers, deeply concerned to present a viewpoint and a method by which men bound fast to the chain of transmigration and in the clutches of the law of Karma might escape and be free from this bondage forever. They were convinced Vedantists, even though they differed widely in their interpretations. But they were not the only philosophers nor was Vedanta the only school of thought. Six systems (darshanas) were worked out and have come down through the centuries. The oldest, the Sankhya, was probably in existence at the time of the Buddha (five hundred years before our era). It differs greatly from most of the others in being atheistic, and yet it has had great influence on Indian thinking ever since it was propounded. It scarcely seems necessary here to list and describe all these systems, two of which scarcely deserve to be called philosophies at all. Indians, with what Hogg speaks of as an "inherent tendency to syncretism," state quite positively that these six systems are six facets of one great reservoir of truth and are not to be considered as contradictory, a conclusion very difficult for a Western thinker to

[2] P. 208. (Italics are mine.)

appreciate or accept. Be that as it may, there are several likenesses which are highly important. They are all philosophies of salvation, calculated to lead men to escape the necessity of being reborn times without number; and they all teach that knowledge is the key to unlock the door, that by knowledge they shall be saved from the thralldom to the power of Karma.

In order, however, to come to a proper appreciation of the place of the Vedanta as a means of release and of its full impact upon the Indian mind, it is necessary to see the Vedanta as only one of the three ways or methods of salvation. These are as follows: "the way of deeds" or "works" (Karma Marga), "the way of loving devotion" (Bhakti Marga), and "the way of knowledge" (Jnana Marga).

A lengthy and authoritative book by Mrs. Sinclair Stevenson entitled *The Rites of the Twice-Born* deals entirely with the first of these ways. Her words summarize the significance of this path:

> But in this book we have chosen the humblest of all the paths, a Way that at its highest never leads its followers to complete Liberation, but only to the passing bliss of a Heaven which he will one day have to leave again. It is, however, the road that most of the simple folk—the ordinary people—amongst the Twice-born are treading; the Way of Rites and Ceremonies.[3]

By the faithful performance of the rules and regulations of the various codes and law books, by holding fast to caste and scrupulously observing caste regulations, by punctiliously following the many rules laid down for worship, a man or woman may build up "good Karma" and look forward to a reward in the next life in a happier state than in the present. It is called Karma Marga because the primary meaning of "Karma" is

[3] P. xvi. Used by permission of Oxford University Press.

"deed" or "act"; here it is an act or a deed which reaps a reward in another life. Of course it works both ways, evil deeds bringing an undesirable penalty. Any deed, good or bad, adds to the quantity of Karma and requires another birth.

We turn to the second of the ways, the way of bhakti, or "loving devotion"; and here there is a far more fascinating story to tell. Now we come into the circle of the Vedanta, for the father of this important movement was the philosopher Ramanuja. To be a Vedantist one must hold to some kind of unity in the universe, and this Ramanuja did. But in the unity to which he held, distinctions were posited, distinctions which were not to be obliterated by absorption or identification in the sole ultimate Reality. Three units make up our universe—a personal deity, a material universe, and individual human beings. This made possible relations between deity and people which are very much like those between Allah and Muslims and God the Father and Christians, a situation which is poles apart from the system of Shankara.

Ramanuja gave philosophic expression to the ideas which were cherished by many, so is looked upon as the real author of bhakti. The Vedanta of Shankara had no room for devotion to a deity, for piety and love; its exponents would say that these attitudes were on a lower level and might be condoned among the masses who could not attain the heights of Vedantic thinking. In opposition Ramanuja set up a system in which worship and loving devotion were given an important place. His appeal was to the emotions and hence had a wide popular following. For several hundreds of years, that is, from his time—the twelfth century—to the period of one of the finest spirits produced by the movement, Tukaram, in the seventeenth century, the bhaktas, adepts in bhakti, were the dominant force in Hinduism. Of course the more rigid form of Vedanta did not die out; it waged constant warfare against the bhaktas and in the end won out.

Bhakti became the doctrine of the Vaishnavas, one of the two great sects into which Hinduism is roughly divided. The great deity is Vishnu, known as a lesser god in the *Rig-Veda* but coming to the fore and occupying today a place of pre-eminence which he shares with one other deity only, Shiva. Vishnu is worshiped not in his own person but in that of one or another of the avatars, or "descents" of Vishnu sent to aid men and women in their need. There are said to be ten of these avatars, by far the most important of which are Rama and Krishna. These two, particularly Krishna, are of the highest importance in popular Hinduism. Avatars have been called "incarnations," like that of God who became incarnate in Jesus Christ in Christian theology; but there are striking dissimilarities. Avatars are temporary manifestations of divinity; Jesus Christ is the one, unchanging revelation of God. We can know what the Christian God is like by studying his incarnation in Christ; it is hard to discover what Vishnu is like by paying attention to his avatars. They are animals as well as manlike creatures. No wonder Godfrey E. Phillips speaks of them as "disguises" and not true likenesses or real incarnations. In his own words, "The Avatars are not incarnations (as the term has been mistranslated) but descents of the divine into the human, or even the subhuman, involving no real assumption of a human nature, even when, as in the stories of Rama and Krishna, the human form is worn for years together." [4]

A likeness to Christianity is to be found in the bhakti conception of God as a gracious being who in his love shows his grace toward men and women in need. God is here the initiator,

⁴ *The Gospel in the World*, pp. 75, 138-39.

seeking those who will come to him for help. Would that we might stop just here in thinking of the bhakti movement and its influence. The appeal to the emotions is always dangerous— in Christianity as well as in other religions—unless it is closely linked to clear thinking as to the nature of the object of worship and is under the strict control of high moral principles. Unfortunately bhakti in practice is very frequently little better than emotionalism run wild. The Hindu writers of *The Cultural Heritage of India* declare that "Bhakti is not of the nature of knowledge. In fact they posit that as the devotee grows in his *Bhakti* experience, his knowledge decreases. 'It is not judgement of the intellect, but an emotion of affection.' It is more than faith, it is burning faith in God." [5]

The more serious fact is that the emotions which are played upon, while often pure and noble, are at times and all too frequently frankly sensual; and hence the worship cannot be uplifting. Of Vallabha (fifteenth and sixteenth centuries A.D.) we read that he held that "release comes with knowledge, seeing the vanity of the world, by devotion and meditation and love of God";[6] and yet this ardent devotee also taught that the performance of the act of coitus was not only a great help but necessary to a spiritual realization.[7] Chaitanya, the Vaishnava devotee of Bengal (sixteenth century), was on a higher level than Vallabha. His life was a continuous frenzy of devotion to Krishna. "His life," says one Bengali admirer, "was a course of thanksgiving, tears, hymns, and praises offered to God." [8] His own life was pure in act though he was willing to allow that imagining sexual scenes and acts was a helpful stimulus to

[5] Immanuel, *op. cit.*, p. 149.
[6] R. G. Bhandarkar, *Vaishnavism, Saivism and Minor Religious Systems*, p. 78.
[7] See Nicol Macnicol, *Indian Theism*, p. 128.
[8] *Ibid.*, p. 131.

devotion. "The sports of Krishna go on always, as the rising and the setting of the sun. . . . Krishna's chief power is that which creates dilation of the heart, or joy. This appears to be the power of love." [9]

With relief we turn to other bhaktas on a very much higher level. There are a number of these men, of whom the most notable was Tukaram (seventeenth century). He worshiped a male deity only, condemning the worship of goddesses. His God is served by devoted love only, and to see God our desires must be restrained. Tukaram cried out to God to help him restrain his passions. He was afraid of becoming conceited and losing humility, so he came to speak of the "death of self in him." [10] Together with a number of other bhaktas Tukaram worshiped one God only. In the words of the Hindu Justice Ranade this movement "checked the excesses of polytheism. It tended in all these ways to raise the nation generally to a higher level of capacity, both of thought and action." [11] With the death of Tukaram the great power of the bhakti movement seems to have spent itself. Of course it continues to exist and exert a strong influence today as one of the three ways of salvation in Hinduism, but no notable bhaktas have appeared for several centuries who are on the level with those just mentioned. It is another kind of personage with a different message who now commands the attention of the educated Hindu.

And now before turning our attention to the newer movement, it must be made clear again that what the Hindu is searching for is release, escape from the shackles of Karma, and also that the two methods of release, by works and devotion, do not

[9] Bhandarkar, op. cit., p. 85. See also M. T. Kennedy, *The Chaitanya Movement in Relation to Christianity*, for full discussion.
[10] Bhandarkar, op. cit., p. 97.
[11] *Rise of the Maratha Power*, p. 171.

and cannot bring one to the final goal. After most scrupulous care in keeping all the rules and regulations laid down by custom and after he has given himself in utter devotion to a deity as a faithful bhakta, he is only assured a happier lot in the next life. It may possibly be in one of a number of heavens, portrayed in glowing colors; but always, whatever his condition, he knows full well that he must die and be reborn again, and thus take up the weary and uncertain round of lives, unless—and here we come to the way of salvation by knowledge, which is the one sure way out of his predicament.

The way of knowledge is the Vedantic method of final deliverance from the dreaded necessity of being reborn again and again according to the law of Karma. It is based upon the preliminary acceptance of the doctrine that there is only one ultimate Reality, Brahman, the Absolute, and that human beings in their essential nature are identical with Brahman. Men are not to look forward to a time when they will be or become Brahman; they are that now. Nor does this doctrine mean that human beings are a part of Brahman; they are each one of them all there is of Brahman—there is complete identification. Now if a man accepts this doctrine and knows this identification to be a fact, a present reality, what more is there for him to do or experience or be? Here we come to one of the most important features of the whole Vedantic system. We may "know" a thing intellectually with our thinking mind, but that is not the kind of knowing which brings release. There is a knowing of another kind, the Vedantist speaking of it as "realization." This realization is attained by intuition, or mystical insight, an achievement in which the mind as we think of it with its functions of intellection, willing, and feeling ceases to operate. By another route he comes to a kind of "knowledge" which is not the knowledge of the intellect but something beyond the intelligible. What he arrives at is his true "essential self," himself as he really is underneath everything else.

It is quite apparent that this attainment is not possible for the ordinary man, busy all day with securing a livelihood for himself and his family. So that when the Vedantist declares that all men are divine and that they will all ultimately attain the goal of realization, it is very evident that there will be many rebirths before this aim can be achieved. In fact most of mankind are not at the stage where they can even know that there is such a realization, let alone seek to achieve it. For them the only course is to give themselves to the ordinary practices of popular Hinduism. Realization is for the recluse, the celibate monk, the devotee who has time and the will to undertake traveling the long way to final release. As one can see at once, discipline is involved, a discipline of the body and of the mind, which will bring the mental concentration without which achievement is not possible. Here we come to the somewhat loosely used word "Yoga."

Yoga is listed as one of the six systems of Hindu philosophy, a system propounded by an ancient seer, Patanjali.[12] Scarcely worthy to be called a philosophical system, Yoga is really a code of physical and mental discipline. First there must be complete physical control, and this means severe and long training.[13] To be able to sit absolutely quiet hours at a time seems almost impossible to the neophyte. This, however, is not the final achievement; it is only a means to an end. Only by having attained efficiency in physical control can the disciple hope to learn the art of mental control, a far more difficult matter.

[12] See Swami Prabhavananda and Christopher Isherwood, How to Know God: The Yoga Aphorisms of Patanjali (1953).
[13] See Theos Bernard, Hatha Yoga, giving his own experience under instruction in India.

Here the aim is concentration. The would-be adept must be able to rid his mind of all the sensations which come to him from the outer world. Then he is to enter the state when all discursive thinking, all mental cogitation, ceases. That is, he passes out of the realm of logical thinking and reasoning according to the ordinary rules of thought. He is entering the region of mystical intuition, of direct grasp of reality; he is becoming his real, essential self, and in that state the flash of intuitive insight occurs. He cries out, "I am That"; he has realized that he is Brahman, that there is no distinction between himself and Ultimate Reality. This is not the final state, for his body is still alive. As long as he continues on this earth, he must live a normal physical and mental life. At intervals, however, he may and does enter the state of intuitive reality when again the world is as if it did not exist.

This is the teaching of Shankara and of the Ramakrishna Mission, Nothing is more instructive than the experience of Sri Ramakrishna Paramahamsa himself. The account which follows is taken from *Sri Ramakrishna, His Unique Message* by Swami Ghanananda, a monk of the order. Before he came to the time of final attainment, Sri Ramakrishna had reached a high level of moral control. A part of the discipline of purification was to give up the

eight-fold fetters of hatred, shame, pedigree, culture, fear, fame, caste and egoism when calling on God. . . . He rooted out the sexual and acquisitive instincts . . . lust and lucre—by peculiar but remarkable processes. . . . He had trained himself so perfectly in this conquest of and desire for and sense of possession that his fingers used to get twisted at the mere touch of a single coin! . . . His marriage is unique in the history of saints, and is the only true example of what has been called spiritual marriage of souls without any carnal taint.

He also gave himself to and passed through the experience of bhakti: "He therefore attempted to explore the realms of *bhakti* or devotion to God, to which the one and only avenue is love."

Sri Ramakrishna came finally to the last stage, the realization of "Pure Consciousness." Says Swami Ghanananda, "The non-dualistic discipline is the most difficult of all spiritual practices. In it all mentation stops and the ego is transcended. The state— if state it can be called—of contentless consciousness is then realized." This final stage was reached under the tutelage of an experienced guru, or spiritual guide. After going through several ceremonies and receiving instruction in the meaning of Vedanta, Sri Ramakrishna was asked "to withdraw the mind completely from all objects and dive into the Atman (Self)." It took him some time to rid his mind of all external objects; but when that was achieved, his mind "at once soared beyond the relative plane and I lost myself in *Samadhi* (superconsciousness)!" The account continues:

The body became motionless like a corpse. The senses and the mind ceased to function. The universe disappeared, and space melted away. Everything was reduced to ideas, which floated like shadows in the dim background of the mind. Only the faint consciousness of "I" repeated itself in dull monotony. Presently that too stopped, and only Existence remained. The soul lost itself in the Self. All idea of duality, of subject and object, was effaced. Sri Ramakrishna realized the *Brahman* (the Absolute).[14]

In this state he remained for three days, at the end of which the guru found him in his room

in the same position in which he had left him. There was no manifestation of life in the body, but the countenance was calm, serene

[14] Pp. 83, 73-74, 75, 111, 138, 142, 143-44. Used by permission of Sri Ramakrishna Math.

and radiant . . . again and again he touched the disciple's corpse-like body. He found no sign of life or consciousness. . . . He at once took steps to bring the mind of Sri Ramakrishna to the relative plane. . . . Little by little the disciple came to the consciousness of the outside universe.[15]

For months after this shattering experience he would re-enter the state of utter unconsciousness to the things of sense. At last he became convinced that he should " 'remain on the threshold of relative consciousness for the sake of humanity. . . . Thus only did the mind gradually come down to a lower level and the consciousness of the body. I became a normal man. But before that at the slightest opportunity the mind would take a transcendental flight and merge in the *nirvikalpa samadhi* [contentless consciousness].' " [16] This experience occurred in 1864. Sri Ramakrishna lived until 1886, the twenty-two years being spent mostly in the company of a group of disciples who gathered around him. India has produced no more remarkable religious character in modern times—it may be in any time in the past. It is small wonder that in the Benares headquarters of the Mission monks and admiring visitors worship the image of this saint placed in a conspicuous location in the grounds.

Considerable space has been given to describe the supreme experience of Sri Ramakrishna, for in no other way has it seemed possible to present so vividly and correctly the meaning of the final attainment of nondualistic Vedanta as in the experience of its most noted and typical devotee in modern times. Others have attained the state of realization, but none that we know of has had it reported so dramatically and with so detailed an exposition.

Sri Ramakrishna, as we have seen, was a man of singularly

[15] *Ibid.*, pp. 144-45. See also Swami Nikhilananda, *Ramakrishna: Prophet of New India.*
[16] *Ibid.*, pp. 147-48.

pure and noble character. The members of the order of monks who bear his name have the reputation of being under strict moral discipline and live lives of unselfish devotion to their fellow men. But with all that—and it must not be discredited by anything which follows—there is unfortunate moral confusion in what they teach; and this has in their labors results which seriously limit the scope of their message and work. In the midst of the description of the experience of Sri Rama-krishna as a bhakta, Swami Ghanananda makes this observation, "Love works in lower or higher planes. The thief robs and the philanthropist spends his wealth in charity. The sinner sins and the saint is godlike. But behind all these there is the working of one and the same motive force called love, though expressing itself in different and sometimes opposite directions." [17] To assert that the thief in doing violence to another by despoiling his property is motivated by love is surely to display moral obliquity of the most serious nature unless of course love is equated with desire, and then we are on a much lower plane. From a slightly different angle we find Swami Nirvedananda saying:

Sins are no more than mistakes committed through ignorance. For such sins one has, of course, to pay by suffering pain here or hereafter. However, he grows wiser through such sufferings and proceeds through repeated births till the Divinity within him is completely manifested. Everyone is to reach this blessed goal. Sinners, therefore, are not to be condemned. They should be treated with sympathy and helped out of ignorance.[18]

While Hinduism in all its forms has a doctrine of salvation, it is putting the thought very mildly when it is asserted that Hinduism, including the Vedanta, has no message of salvation

[17] *Ibid.*, p. 112.
[18] *Hinduism at a Glance*, 2nd ed., p. 212.

from sin. Not only so, but what hope has the Ramakrishna Mission for the sinner to help him on his feet and make him into a new man? What about the thief, or what is worse, the mean man, the selfish man, the bully in his own home, the murderer, the impure man—are we to look at him hopelessly and comfort ourselves with the hope that in the future after a long succession of rebirths he will ultimately come to a realization of the divinity within? That seems to be about as far as the Vedantist can go. He has no enabling gospel of present help for the sinner; he cannot envisage the drunkard turned by divine grace into a sober man. Alcoholics Anonymous with its message of hope could get no encouragement from the Hindu, for he sees no way by which a man can throw off his bondage. The Ramakrishna Mission is a mission to the respectable people of a community but could scarcely organize a mission to the slums and the down-and-outs.

Closely connected with this attitude toward evil and wrongdoing is the fatal lack of the need for and possibility of a doctrine of repentance and forgiveness. The doctrine of Karma nullifies any such thought. Every evil deed must receive its appropriate punishment to the last ounce. There is no mitigation and no release. The Vedantist would declare that forgiveness is immoral because it makes light of the seriousness of evil by canceling its requital. That might be true if the person remained the same and continued to harbor evil desires and purposes. But in Christianity repentance and forgiveness are transforming; they create a complete change of mind and heart, so that we are dealing with an entirely new and different situation. A new man emerges, so that he comes to love the things he once hated and hates the things he once loved. Even as between men true repentance-and-forgiveness becomes one of the most constructive forces in human life. When forgiveness is seen in its Christian garb as being the restoration of a broken relationship between two parties, the aggrieved and the one who has done him evil, there is nothing more wonderful than that experience. The genuine experience always means an inner transformation, made possible by true repentance on the part of one and genuine forgiveness on the part of the other.

An illustration of the difference between the two attitudes just mentioned is at hand. Japanese Buddhism came to that country through Korea and China from India. The differences between the Buddhist sects in Japan and Hinduism and early Buddhism in India are striking, and yet there are likenesses. At no point can this be seen more clearly than in the hold of the doctrine of rebirth and Karma in Japan as well as in India. Shinsho Hanayama, a member of the faculty of the National University in Tokyo and at the same time a priest of the Jodo sect of Buddhism, was requested to act as chaplain of the Japanese war prisoners in the Sugamo prison in Tokyo and for three years was in close contact with the condemned prisoners. He has published a book describing his experiences and giving intimate details of his relations with the men and their attitudes.[19] In this volume the striking thing from the Christian point of view is that in the revelation of their religious views these prisoners give no indication that there was any need for repentance because of what they had done and consequently no place for forgiveness. Yet in their confessions the explanation of what they were and had done was laid to what they had been; in other words, that they were under the control of the law of Karma. Nor did Hanayama as a Buddhist priest even approach his charges with the thought that they had anything to repent of or that they were in need of forgiveness.

On the other hand, we have a very different picture in that

---

[19] *The Way of Deliverance* (1950).

of the German prisoners convicted of war crimes by the court which met at Nuremberg. An extended article by Henry F. Gerecke is entitled "I Walked to the Gallows with the Nazi Chiefs." [20] The caption under the title states that "now, after five years under a bond of silence, he tells how they repented before the hangman's trap fell." Much stress was laid on the necessity of genuine repentance before the prisoners were admitted to the communion of the Lord's Supper. "More than half of the Nazis there, before going to the gallows or their long imprisonment at Spandau, asked God for forgiveness of their sins against Him and humanity and returned to the Christian faith of their forebears." Some of course like Goering were obdurate until the end. It would be easy to be cynical of the genuineness of their repentance—men facing death would be likely to do what they had learned from the tradition in which they had been reared. But that would be to miss the point. The striking thing is the complete contrast of the position of those under the thrall of Karma and those who know the Christian way. The Christian teaching of a heavenly Father who is both righteous and loving and who seeks to forgive and bring back the sinner to fellowship with himself is an essential part of the gospel of Christ and causes his religion to stand out in contrast to Buddhism, which is dominated by the law of Karma.

Again, the salvation which the Vedantist proclaims is to be achieved by human beings by their own efforts. The doctrine of the grace of God, which finds large place in the teaching of the bhakti leaders, is left entirely behind; and man achieves his emancipation by his own tedious following of the way of knowledge. There is no help from without. This means that there is no true worship in Vedanta teaching, no prayer for help, no need of the mercy and power of God. Brahman is not a "prayer hearing and a prayer answering" God but the attributeless Absolute who literally cannot think about and care for those who are struggling to attain the great goal of existence.

What is the state of those who have attained realization, men like Sri Ramakrishna and many others? The immediate answer is that they will never be reborn again. The law of Karma is nullified; it ceases to operate. This alone raises the teaching about realization to a most important level in Vedanta. The statement has been repeated several times that with all that the way of works and the way of loving devotion may accomplish, it has no effect upon the operation of the law of Karma. A man may hope for a more pleasant lot in another life by doing good deeds and being devoted to his deity, but he is still under an inexorable law. He must pay the last ounce of retribution for evil as well as reap the full reward for the good he has done. But now at last, in realizing that he is identical with Brahman, he passes beyond the operation of that law.

Again we must be reminded that he is no longer in any danger of being punished in one or another of the hells of popular religion, nor has he any prospect of enjoying a beatific life in a heaven. He has passed out of the region of heavens and hells, of rewards and punishments. He does not become any more of what Brahman is by the transition through which he has passed. He *is* Brahman and has *always* been Brahman. No change of status as a man has taken place. He is essentially what he has always been. The only difference lies in the fact that he now recognizes or realizes what he is as formerly he did not. It is illumination in place of former ignorance. Liberation, or "moksha,"

is the realization of That which has existed from eternity but has hitherto been concealed from us. . . . He who knows the Self is liberated; even the gods cannot prevent his being so, because he has realized himself to be the very Soul (Atman) of the gods. . . . He has attained the true Immortality, that is to say, indestructibility without a continued existence, and not the state of non-dying-ness in heaven.[21]

But how does a liberated soul, a jivanmukta [one liberated while living], act? Swami Nikhilananda has this to say, "Ordinary minds cannot understand his actions, life, or movements, any more than a dreaming man can see the world of the awakened." [22] He no longer, even while in this life, is under the sway of his past actions. Thus Karma is nullified not only in the release of the liberated from the dread of rebirth but also in their freedom from the effects of deeds in former lives. "Evil does not overtake him, but he transcends all evil. Evil does not trouble him, [but] he consumes all evil. He becomes sinless, taintless, free from doubts, and a knower of Brahman." [23]

All the way through the writings of Vedantists an analogy is made use of which is very suggestive. It is found in the three phases of human consciousness with which we are all familiar. We are fully conscious when we are awake, we have a kind of consciousness when we dream in sleep, though it is vagrant and uncontrolled, but what about dreamless sleep? That is declared to be a genuine form of consciousness. Swami Nikhilananda has this to say, "In the state of deep sleep the soul does not really become unconscious. The Consciousness belonging to Atman is not destroyed, because this Consciousness is immortal. It appears, therefore, that in the relative world [life in this material world] the nearest approach to the peace and desirelessness of Brahman is the experience of deep sleep." [24]

[21] Nikhilananda, *The Upanishads*, I, 103. Used by permission of Harper & Bros.
[22] *Ibid.*, p. 105.
[23] *Brihadaranyaka Upanishad*, IV. iv. 23.
[24] *Op. cit.*, p. 94.

One further question remains to be asked: What becomes of the liberated soul when the body dies? To put it in the words of Swami Nikhilananda, "Whither will the soul of the knower of Atman go? It does not go to any place where it has not been from the very beginning, nor does it become anything other than what it has always been—that is to say, Brahman, Pure Consciousness." [25] Is every question answered by that answer? "Pure Consciousness"—what does that phrase mean? The only analogy we have to help us to understand any kind of consciousness is our own waking consciousness, and yet we are told that Pure Consciousness, or Super Consciousness, is as different from our waking consciousness as is our state when we are in dreamless sleep as contrasted with our state when we are fully awake. It has been stated that the condition of a man who is emancipated and has left this life is just as if he were in a state of dreamless sleep from which he will never awake. That would probably not satisfy the Vedantist. There is always a plus in an analogy. Jesus used the analogy of human fatherhood when he spoke of God as Father. What he meant was that those qualities in a great and good human father were correct pointers toward what God was like, only there was the inevitable plus— God was like a human father but was very much more, both in greatness and in goodness. The qualities in the human father served only to point in the right direction toward what God was like. But those words "in the right direction" are of prime importance. There is a real analogy, a real likeness, a similarity between the human father and God; or the analogy would cease to be such, the words would be meaningless. It is difficult to avoid the conclusion that to use the word "consciousness" of the state of man in deep, dreamless sleep or of Brahman or of man as Brahman cannot convey meaning or sense to a man

[25] *Ibid.*, p. 104.

possessed of human consciousness, for by definition Brahman is ineffable. Human language is simply incapable of carrying meaning of that which has no analogy with what is in the experience of mortal man.

Attention has been called to the ascription to Brahman of the qualities of existence, consciousness, bliss (sat, chit, ananda); but it is also carefully explained that these are not positive but merely negative terms, so that they do not negate the necessary dogma that Brahman the Absolute is attributeless. So again the word "consciousness" does not carry us far in our search for the meaning of what Brahman is like and what men who have been liberated are like when their bodies die. It is not an altogether happy allusion when Swami Nikhilananda speaks of the "boredom of heaven" when the prospect which he has to offer the liberated is spoken of as "contentless." No one can picture the world to come without the use of analogies drawn from the earth and earthly conditions. The "gates of pearl" and the "streets of gold" in our traditional imagery are only analogies and not descriptions of a truly spiritual world. But when it is possible to speak of fellowship with God and with the redeemed, we have a real analogy. We know what fellowship means here on earth, and that points to a fellowship above—again there is the big plus, but it points in the right direction. So the Christian has a lively hope of real life which will be filled with far more than he enjoys under mundane conditions here below. "Contentless consciousness" has little to commend itself to living men and women as contrasted with "fellowship" with the God of love and righteousness, and companionship with the company of the redeemed who have been transformed into the likeness of God as we see it in Christ Jesus.

137

Chapter Seven

Are All the Religions Alike?

As I walked out of the grounds of the Ramakrishna Mission in Benares, a fine-looking and friendly monk greeted me with the question, "You are a Christian, are you not?" On receiving an affirmative reply he made this statement, "We too believe in Christianity; we celebrate Christmas and Good Friday and Easter," thus giving expression to one of the fundamental teachings of the Mission. As it is stated in their official pronouncements, "Vedanta accepts all the religions of the world, because it recognizes the same divine inspiration in all." [1]

Not only is this one of the characteristic doctrines of the Ramakrishna Mission, but it has become current among the Hindu intelligentsia. On the second anniversary of Indian independence a public official in Jabalpur in the course of a patriotic address incidentally remarked, "Of course all religions are alike; they say that there are differences in the dogmas of the different religions, but they amount to nothing," and the gesture with which he tossed off these differences emphasized their meaninglessness to him. It was seemingly a chance remark, having little or no connection with the main current of his address; but this very fact brings out the axiomatic character of the statement as it has come to be recognized by educated men in every part of the land.

Undoubtedly this attitude had been in circulation before his time, but we must look to the experience and practice of Sri Ramakrishna Paramahamsa for enthusiastic acceptance of the

[1] Vedanta in America.

idea and its inclusion in the teaching which he imparted to his followers. One of these disciples of the present generation, speaking of his master's work, is convinced that "his message of the Harmony of Religions forms his greatest contribution to spiritual thought." [2]

It behooves us then to look carefully at this aspect of the life of Sri Ramakrishna. He was a mystic, the supreme mystic of all time, according to the estimate of his devotees, who do not hesitate to worship him as worthy of their highest adoration. As already portrayed, he passed through one experience after another until finally he entered into the experience of "Contentless Consciousness, realizing the *Brahman* or the Impersonal Absolute beyond all mentation and all the relationships between subject and object. He had attained that state in which one does not feel one has to gain by doing anything, or loses by not doing." [3] This might be sufficient for any Hindu, but it did not satisfy Sri Ramakrishna, who reached out to try to understand other religions. His method of course was that of mystical experience. Being a man of the most meager education, he does not give evidence of prolonged study in the literature of these faiths. But in India the world's religions are all there, so it was not difficult for him to come into contact with their representatives close at hand. Thus he came to know about Islam, millions of whose votaries lived in his native Bengal. Sri Ramakrishna received a kind of initiation into Islam from a member of a Sufi, or mystical sect, and began to act as a Muslim. In his own words, "Then I used to repeat the name of Allah, dress myself in the fashion of Mohammedans, and recite the Namaz [a liturgical prayer] regularly. All Hindu ideas being wholly

---

[2] Ghanananda, op. cit., p. vi. Used by permission of Sri Ramakrishna Math.
[3] Ibid., p. 150.

banished from the mind, not only did I not salute the Hindu gods and goddesses, but I had no inclination to visit them." [4] But even then his experience as a Muslim worshiper was not complete; his mind immediately passed into the realization of Brahman as a part of his Islamic experience, a strange mixture of Islam and Hinduism.

It was not difficult for Sri Ramakrishna to think of Gautama Buddha as closely related to Hinduism or actually a Hindu. While Buddha initiated a movement which has severed itself completely from Hinduism, all thoughtful Hindus of the present day look on the Buddha as one of themselves. He is actually mentioned as the last avatar, or incarnation of Vishnu, along with Krishna and Rama, who are second to no others of the popular objects of worship.

His experience with Jesus Christ is far more significant, and to bring him into his pantheon of divine beings shows the remarkable ability of Sri Ramakrishna to transcend differences and harmonize quite obvious contradictions. The experience he had was strange and very striking. A serious-minded man, not a Christian, was in the habit of reading the Bible to Sri Ramakrishna. Thus by hearing the Christian scriptures read a desire was awakened in the mind of Sri Ramakrishna to "realize" Christianity as he had Islam. There were several steps in the experience. One day while looking at a picture of the Madonna and the child Jesus, he was filled with admiration "when he felt as though the picture had become animated and that rays of light were emanating from the figures of Mary and Jesus, entering into him and altogether changing his mental outlook." [5] This went beyond what he had expected, so he attempted to turn his mind to his Hindu gods and goddesses but could not

[4] *Ibid.*, pp. 153-54.
[5] *Ibid.*, p. 156.

do so. In great agitation he prayed to the Divine Mother, Kali, to whom he always turned in any time of need; but this did not avail. "A deep regard for Christ and the Christian Church filled his heart." [6] This mood remained with him for days until he had a vision of "an extra-ordinary looking person of serene aspect approaching him with his gaze intently fixed on him." [7] Sri Ramakrishna did not recognize who the figure was until it drew closer. Then he knew, and we hear him exclaiming, "This is the Christ who poured out his heart's blood for the redemption of mankind and suffered agonies for its sake. It is none other than the Master-Yogin Jesus, the embodiment of love." [8] Then we are told that "the Son of Man embraced Sri Ramakrishna and became merged in him. He lost his outward consciousness in samadhi [superconsciousness] realizing his union with the Brahman with attributes. After some time he came back to the normal plane. He became convinced that Jesus Christ was an Incarnation of God." [9] Undoubtedly this was a moving emotional experience in the mind and heart of a deeply earnest and sincere man, but to conclude that Sri Ramakrishna had really entered into the meaning of Christ and the Christian faith is impossible for one who has any understanding of the New Testament.

Sri Ramakrishna had similar though not as striking experiences with the so-called founders of Jainism and with certain gurus, leaders of Sikhism. We can now understand how it came about that after passing through these experiences and believing that he understood other religions by immediate experience, this man should come to the conclusion that all the religions

[6] Ibid.
[7] Ibid., p. 157.
[8] Ibid.
[9] Ibid., pp. 157-58.

were true, so that no one should ever be invited to leave one religion and turn to another. He was quite consistent and set up images of the various divine beings with whom he had come into rapport and would worship them in turn or as he felt inclined at any time. And yet in and through all that he did and thought, Sri Ramakrishna remained a Hindu to the core and was ready to defend every feature of Hinduism no matter how incongruous it might be with his other beliefs.

The charge is made that while the Vedanta is broad-minded and liberal in looking upon every religion as true and worthy, Christianity in contrast is narrow-minded, dogmatic, intolerant, and exclusive. Christianity does not look upon all religions as essentially alike or true while the Vedanta does. This charge demands close scrutiny. So far as being dogmatic, it would seem that Christianity and Vedanta are alike. Christianity has certain doctrines which are considered essential, without which it would cease to exist as a distinct, separate religion, but is this not the case also with Vedanta? It may seem to be liberal in its belief that all religions are true and lead to the same goal, but this very belief hardens into a dogma so essential that without it the Vedanta of the Ramakrishna Mission would be bereft of one of the most significant and appealing features of its message. Says Swami Akhilananda, "The very life of Sri Ramakrishna is an interpretation and validification of that ancient Vedic teaching that 'Truth is one,' " [10] which is taken to mean that all religions are one and the same. This is believed and proclaimed as tenaciously and confidently as any Christian doctrine. Moreover, everything in their attitude, including that toward other faiths, is directly related to an even more fundamental doctrine; namely, that there is a unifying principle in

[10] *Hindu View of Christ*, p. 276. Used by permission of Philosophical Library, Inc.

the universe, the Absolute Brahman. Even more than this, Brahman, as we have seen, is held to be the final reality in the universe. Without this doctrine the Vedantists would be shorn of the most characteristic and determinative feature in their thinking. To realize that human beings are identical with Brahman is their distinctive message, without which there would be little or nothing to hold them together as a group with a common belief and a common purpose—hence the dogmatic insistence on the necessity of accepting this doctrine.

But let us look at the charge that Christianity is exclusive. There is certainly a sense in which it is a valid charge. Our religion is built upon the claim that the one God of the universe revealed himself to men in Jesus Christ and that he is the one Saviour and Lord of men. This place of pre-eminent authority can be occupied by one and only one being. To use one of his own sayings in the Gospels, "No man can serve two masters" (Matt. 6:24). If it were true that religion is basically the acceptance of a body of beliefs or the practice of a set of laws or regulations, it would not be unreasonable to aim at a synthesis of some kind, but such is not the case in Christianity. Our religion is at bottom a loyalty or a commitment to a person, an allegiance to Jesus Christ not only as Saviour but as Lord and Master of our lives. We give ourselves to him completely as the one source of our very lives as Christians. There can be no thought of dividing loyalty among a number of masters—that would be a psychological impossibility in the very nature of the case. We cannot be completely devoted to more than one, and all Christian teaching stems from him and what he does for us. This undoubtedly is exclusive, and we are glad to have it known.

Sometimes, however, the term "exclusive" is extended to cover far more than this primary commitment. It comes to mean narrowness and even intolerance, a narrowness which can see no good in other religions and which at times runs into the attitude which at its worst has resulted in scorn and persecution. Christians are sometimes said to refuse to have fellowship with men of good will and sincerity of other faiths even when these men are working for the good of humanity. This narrowness is not willing to see and acknowledge any good in other systems and give them credit for purity of motive and actual accomplishment in raising human life to higher levels and in giving men hope and faith in a worthy ideal. There are, unfortunately, those in the Christian ranks who are thus minded, who close their minds tightly against any such acknowledgment and make unwarranted charges against those who differ from them. But happily the number of those otherwise minded is large and growing. The science of the history of religion and the comparative study of religions have cleared their minds of many misconceptions, and they are glad to discover and give full weight to the noble men who have appeared along the way and who have enriched humanity by their example and their teaching.

An analogy may be useful at this point. One might say that Christianity is as exclusive as the ideal in Christian marriage. And how exclusive Christian marriage is! "Forsaking all other keep thee only unto her, so long as ye both shall live"—so runs the formula in the ritual of the marriage ceremony. Could anything be more exclusive? It is a binding obligation recognized by both church and state. And yet tens of thousands enter the married state every year with no sense of doing an incongruous thing—and why? Yes, we have the words of Christ and the attitudes given expression to by the apostle Paul, and these are sufficient backing in the minds of most for the taking of vows so exclusive and binding. But it is also recognized that the scriptural injunctions are based on deep factors in human

144

nature, that the dignity of human personality is preserved by this exclusiveness as is not possible in a polygamous relation. Neither man nor woman can come to the realization of the meaning of life at its deepest and best without that sense of confidence and assurance which comes from faith in the complete loyalty of one to the other in the closest of all human relationships. And in addition this is the only basis on which a Christian home can be established and a family founded with its necessary unity and cohesion. The love and loyalty of father and mother for each other become the foundation on which love and devotion among the children can be taught and exemplified.

And yet at the same time this life commitment, which is surely and designedly exclusive, does not carry with it the stigma of narrowness. The Christian family is as far removed as it is possible to imagine from the kind of exclusiveness which is found in the harem and zenana, where wives are secluded behind the purdah and have no opportunity to enjoy and profit by contact with the society of men as well as women outside their own immediate family circle. Without these contacts women develop blighted lives warped by restrictions which cramp and dwarf their minds and hearts. There is no such exclusiveness in Christian marriage. Great freedom exists, and so much is this the rule that we rarely stop to consider its significance— the freedom of wholesome friendship between men and women, and of co-operation in worth-while tasks too numerous to mention. This is the Christian ideal and practice. It came out of Christianity and follows the expansion of the Christian ideal far and wide over the world. And all this is practiced without lessening in the slightest degree the basic fidelity of husband and wife.

Why, then, cannot Christians come out on the broad liberal

platform of belief in the essential likeness of the great faiths of mankind? For the simple reason that to do so would run contrary to the commitment of the Christian to his Saviour and Lord. He could as soon become a polygamist. The very gist of Christianity lies in this commitment and loyalty to its Master. Christianity is built on the revelation of God in Christ Jesus, who acted on our behalf in giving his life on the cross. He thus made it possible for men to enter into a new life. Because Christ is the manifestation in the flesh of the one God of the universe, he becomes our Lord and has the right to our complete loyalty. So to put all religions on the same level means to disregard that which makes our religion what it is in any distinctive and recognizable form.

It is quite otherwise in the Vedanta, whose attitude is controlled by an entirely different concept. As we have seen, all the religions of the world are to the Vedantist unreal and cease to function when men are emancipated from the ignorance which now controls them and when they come into the realization that there is only one reality and that is Brahman the Absolute. So it is easy to be liberal and broad-minded in this attitude toward various objects of worship. Such a belief does not touch the deep foundation on which the Vedanta is built and consequently is not a matter of life and death for Vedantists. On the other hand, should one ask them to make belief in Brahman optional, they must of necessity refuse, for the reason that their very existence would be jeopardized and they would have no message to declare.

Surely the question must have occurred to the reader as to what the Vedantists mean when they declare that all religions are alike. Is it not evident from even a cursory survey of the religions of mankind that there are many differences, some of which penetrate to the very heart of the various systems? Men

146

of learning like S. Radhakrishnan are quite ready to admit that differences are to be found but claim that they are not highly significant. He tells us that the religions "must develop a spirit of comprehension," since they are "varied expressions of a single truth." Also, "according to the *Bhagavadgita* the Supreme accepts us as we are, no matter how we approach Him, for all paths in which we may wander are His." He places all religions in the same category when he declares that "no historical religion can be regarded as truth absolute and changeless." He quotes with approval Mohandas Gandhi when he says, "I regard all the great faiths of the world as equally true with my own." [11] Such statements are to be found scattered in the writings of practically all the exponents of neo-Hinduism.

Fortunately we have a volume whose purpose it is to elucidate this viewpoint. It is written by the venerable scholar Bhagavan Das of Benares and is entitled *The Essential Unity of All Religions*, running to more than seven hundred pages in its greatly enlarged second edition. In his "Letter to the Reader" the author recognizes that, as individuals differ, so their views on an important matter like religion must differ also. He looks upon the attempt to trace the differences back to their origins and to compare and evaluate them as an endless task and likely to engender discord and disagreements.

[So] why not then promote religious brotherhood and peace among the general public, by saying at once, what is utterly true also— that all atoms and all mentations and all religions, of all countless generations of living beings, past, present, future . . . are all equally derived from the Universal, Eternal, Body-Mind, Matter-Spirit, God-Nature, the One Omnipotent, Omnipresent, Omniscient Self, in whose Consciousness "all things live and move and have their being" which pervades them all?

[11] *Eastern Religions and Western Thought*, pp. 306, 310, 330, 313.

To continue:

In this All-pervading All-including Mind and Its infinite Ideation, all Religion, Philosophy, Science, Law, Art, meet and merge; and from It they all emerge; in endless repetition. When we come to That, all questions are answered; all doubts are set at rest; the Final Synthesis is achieved; the Final Peace of Mind is gained.[12]

What immediately becomes evident is that Das starts out with an assumption which he takes for granted and which he seems to feel, rather naïvely it would seem to Western readers, will be accepted by all as fundamental truth. On this foundation all religious doctrines must be built to be accepted by mankind as valid. So from the start we are made to realize that no attempt is to be made to discuss the characteristic and distinct features of the great religious systems but something very different. The purpose which Das has in mind is to show how the teachings of the various religions agree with and corroborate the primary affirmation of the Vedanta philosophy. Then with very great industry the author searches through the scriptures of the world's religions to discover evidences which point to the agreement which he feels sure they contain. It would be impossible and unnecessary for our purpose here to present the entire argument and give quotations from one religion after another, as interesting as that would be. All we can do is to pick out some of the statements dealing with quotations from the Christian Scriptures.

At once we come upon a startling declaration: "That there is agreement between the great religions, that all teach the same essential truths, *their promulgators themselves are all agreed*. We have their clear assurance on this point." [13] With

---

[12] *The Essential Unity of All Religions*, pp. xvii-xviii, xix. Used by permission of The Theosophical Press.

[13] *Ibid.*, p. 60. (The italics are mine.)

reference to our Lord we read, "Christ (i.e., 'the anointed with Divine Wisdom') says: 'I come not to destroy the law and the prophets but to fulfill them,' " by which Das means the teachings of the other religions. Again:

The essence of Christianity is the same as that of Dharma Sanskrit for "teaching," "law," or "the way." "Christos" means the "anointed," the "bathed in Divine Wisdom," whence only the replacement of the small self by the Great Self. . . . Christ has said: "I am (i.e., is) the Way, the Truth, and the Life." To know that (the) I (is) am all selves is to know the Truth. To love all selves as my-Self is the right Life. To do unto all selves as to my-Self is the righteous way.

Could there be a better illustration of eisegesis, or faulty interpretation by reading into a text one's own ideas?

That man and God, by which is meant the Absolute Brahman, are essentially one is a cardinal truth in Vedanta. To put it in Das's words, "The one basic Truth of truths is that man is in essence one with God." The attempt is made to show that this is the teaching of the Bible. "Behold, the man has become as one of us" (Gen. 3:22), in which declaration God is the speaker. Also, "I have said, ye are gods; and all of you are children of the most High" (Ps. 82:6). Paul is made to join the chorus which identifies man and God: "Know ye not that ye are the temple of God, and the Spirit of God dwelleth in you?" (I Cor. 3:16).[14] With no consideration of the context or of the background in the Jewish tradition, in which the transcendence of the Almighty is never for a moment left in doubt, our author would twist these—and other—texts away from their primary meaning and make them teach a monism

---

[14] *Ibid.*, pp. 62, 82, 83, 91, 95-96.

or pantheism which is utterly at variance with what any Old or New Testament writer could imagine.

Jesus himself, as he is represented in the Fourth Gospel, is quite readily quoted as being in harmony with Vedanta. Did he not say, "I and my Father are one" (10:30)? The suggestion is not made that this oneness might be unity in purpose, aim, or love. No, it must be a metaphysical oneness, a complete identification of Father and Son without any distinction whatsoever. But Jesus in his high-priestly prayer goes even further; speaking of those who would believe as a result of the preaching of the apostles, he prays, "That they may all be one; even as thou, Father, art in me, and I in thee, that they also may be in us. . . . That they may be one, even as we are one; I in them, and thou in me, that they may be perfected into one." (17:21-23.) Again the word "one" is taken to mean identity and not conscious fellowship, a fellowship in a task based upon moral and spiritual oneness with the Father of all and Jesus Christ, who has made him known. We see in Christ the character of the Father in his concern and love for men. We are to be one with God in will and purpose in order to be able to convince men that he has been made manifest in his Son, Jesus Christ.

With many other quotations from the Bible, Das would convince us that Christianity and Vedantic Hinduism are in agreement in the great affirmation that God and man are one. He also affirms the same likenesses between the Vedanta and other religions. There are hundreds of quotations from the great scriptures of the world in which the likenesses are noted. It is enough to quote a summary statement which gives the author's conclusion: "All religions therefore pre-eminently proclaim the Recognition of the Universal Self." [15] It might be said in passing

[15] *Ibid.*, p. 333.

that it is easy to imagine that the scholarly adherents of one religion after another would rise and disclaim the similarity at this point and that which Das affirms. A Muslim mullah would be as surprised as a Christian scholar when he reads such a passage as this, "It does not appear that the Bible and the Quran contain any explicit affirmation of rebirth. *But they nowhere deny it either.* And Christ said that the prophet Elijah had come again as John the Baptist." [16] The doctrine of the transmigration of souls is, as we have seen, fundamental to the Hinduism of all schools and sects both popular and highly intellectual. But to resort to the device of saying that Christianity and Islam do not deny the doctrine of rebirth in order to press further the claim to likeness between these religions and Hinduism is certainly unconvincing, to say the least. Even a very slight acquaintance with Christianity and Islam is sufficient to demonstrate that the reason why they do not deal with transmigration, either in affirmation or in denial is because the idea is utterly foreign to their entire outlook and did not even occur to their prophets and seers.

On the other hand, it is very evident that there are certain likenesses between Christianity and Hinduism and other religions. It is fundamental to them all to believe in a higher power, by whatever name he or it may be called. Even here there are exceptions. One of these is early Buddhism, flourishing in its Hinayana form in Ceylon, Burma, and Thailand. But here it is hard to distinguish between the reverence which is paid to "Lord Buddha" by the common people and genuine worship to a god or higher power which the Buddha repudiated. About the same is true of the Jain religion in India, whose adherents refuse to be called atheists though they declare that

[16] *Ibid.*, pp. 164-65.

there is no creator God who is the object of their worship. They do, however, pray and offer sacrifices to a number of worthies of long ago whom they call tirthankaras, or "those who show the true way across the troubled ocean of life." But with these exceptions the great religions of the world—and this includes most of the Buddhist sects of China and Japan— are at one in their belief and worship of a higher power or powers. And with that statement men like Bhagavan Das and others who are believers in the oneness of the religions of the world are content and proceed no further. But it is impossible for the Christian to stop here. The religions may be in agreement in the fact of believing in higher powers whom they worship; but the further and equally important question immediately emerges: What are the nature and character of the objects of worship in the various religions? The distinctive characteristic of a religion does not lie in the fact that it worships a god or gods but in the kind of God who is worshiped. It is that which makes a religion what it is. And here the differences are so great that it is meaningless to say that they are all essentially alike because they believe in and worship some deity.

It is important to keep in mind that the Ramakrishna Mission with its fundamental belief in Brahman has set itself to defend all aspects of Hinduism, popular as well as that of the intelligentsia, all except untouchability. And be it said to their honor that in their opposition to the terrible treatment of the fifty or sixty millions of outcastes, or Untouchables, they have set themselves in the strongest contrast with most Hindus in their despite and ill treatment of these most unfortunate and miserable people. But this having been said, it must be added that we find the members of the Mission seeking to give a favorable interpretation of beliefs and practices which can never lift the

Hindu populace to high levels of spirituality and ethical practice.

One illustration is immediately at hand. The favorite deity of Sri Ramakrishna was Kali, whose main center of worship is at the Kalighat, in the city of Calcutta, which was named after this goddess. No devotion could be more sincere and complete than that of Sri Ramakrishna to his "Mother Kali," as he was wont to address her. On all occasions, in difficulty or in illness, in joy and in uncertainty, he would turn to Kali in prayer and praise. She was to him an exalted being, the sum of all virtues and excellence, who seemed able to lift him to heights unattainable otherwise.

One of the most incomprehensible things to us of the West is the ability of the Indian mind to make horrible things seem beautiful, incongruous things seem appropriate and reasonable. We can have no better illustration than just here. What kind of divinity is Kali as worshiped by hundreds of thousands of people in Calcutta and Bengal? With reference to her and her worship no other word seems to fit better than the word "horrible." The image of Kali is that of a woman black in color. She stands upon the body of her husband, the god Shiva, one of the so-called trinity of modern Hinduism; she wears a skirt consisting of human hands and arms cut off just below the elbow; she has a long necklace of human skulls around her neck. This strange being has four arms and hands, in one of which she holds a man's head which she has just cut off, in another the dripping sword with which she has committed the murder, and in another a basin in which to catch the blood from the dripping head; and as one of the most repulsive features, Kali's tongue hangs out eager to be spattered with blood, which she craves. Truly here is a picture of a bloodthirsty, demoniacal terror; and yet such worship goes on today and one can stand, as I have had occasion to do, and watch little goats being decapitated, whose blood was taken into the temple and spattered on the tongue of Kali.

The only excuse for this terrible description is that it gives ample evidence that no uplift can be looked for, spiritually or morally, from such worship. Yes, these people are worshiping a god as we Christians do, but there the likeness ends. Can anyone compare worship of such a deity with worship of the God whose likeness has been revealed in Jesus Christ our Lord without seeing that a celestial diameter separates them? When such comparisons are made, the claim that religions are essentially alike seems to be a complete incongruity.

It is not necessary to go into detail any further; but a study of one other form of worship, that of Krishna, will display features not conducive to high spirituality and noble living. When we read the *Gita*, we find one conception of Krishna; but when we turn to the *Tantras* and the *Puranas*, we realize that there is another. In the one case Krishna is a noble counselor who makes the claim of being worthy of worship, of being equal with the absolute Brahman in all his ineffable glory. Unfortunately this is not the conception in the minds of the vast majority of his worshipers in innumerable shrines and temples all over India. The popular stories which are told by the fireside and repeated a thousand times over in all walks of life are filled with Krishna's amorous dalliance with shepherd maidens on the hills and his adulterous relations with Radha, his mistress, another man's wife. Are religions alike? Only in certain formal aspects; pierce beneath the surface, and they diverge widely, never so much so as Christianity and Hinduism, especially in its more popular forms.

To use an analogy from another phase of human affairs, one might say that all the nations of the world are alike because

154

they all have boundaries, they all have governments, and they all speak languages, to mention only a few of the many similarities. But what have we been doing? Only calling attention to some formal aspects of their life, without which they could not be thought of as nations at all. What do we know about the nations of the world from these statements? Just enough to classify groups of people as nations but nothing as to their character or inner nature. How different is the situation as soon as we ask, *What kind* of government has one nation as compared with another? *What* languages do they speak? Then the differences begin to appear. The nations may be alike in an outward, formal way, in the general pattern which makes it possible to put them in one category of human life and relations, but only so far. Penetrate to the features which make a nation what it is in its individuality, and that nation stands out with startling uniqueness. Surely we cannot but be impressed with this distinction as between the religions of the world. Formally they have likenesses, but in content how different! It is only by failing to be directed to the real differences that men can say that all the religions of the world are essentially alike.[17]

Under the heading "The Golden Rule of Christ," [18] Das has little difficulty in quoting from the scriptures of a number of the religions sayings that are so much alike that he is justified in holding that the Golden Rule, in either a negative or positive form, has been widely accepted as a rule of conduct. But when we come to "The Reason for the Golden Rule," we are amazed to find the following:

[17] For a recent study of this subject see *The Conflict of Religions* by Philip H. Ashby, of Princeton University, in which the claim that all religions are essentially alike is shown to be impossible to maintain.

[18] *Op. cit.*, p. 297.

The Golden Rule is the direct outcome, or complementary aspect, of the ultimate Spiritual Truth of truths. Why should I do unto others as I would be done by? Because "I" and "others" are all one I, One Universal Self; because, therefore, what I do to others I do to myself, in and through those "others," and "sins" as well as good deeds, "come home to roost," so that, soon or late, "As I do unto others, so it shall be done to me." [19]

So altruism, or unselfish devotion to others, ceases to be altruism and becomes self-interest; and essential selfishness becomes the rule of life.

A long section in the volume by Das is devoted to a consideration of other similarities in the great religions.[20] All men not only believe in some higher power, but all worship and pray; they have their moral codes; they do wrong and feel that it is necessary to do something about it; they believe in revelation, that their gods make known their will to men; they use images, have forms of worship, go on pilgrimages, and have sacraments of one kind or another—these are among the items in the list. But as one reads, the conviction deepens that the similarities, at least between Hinduism and Christianity, are likenesses in outward form only and not in inner content. To take one example, that of revelation, A. G. Hogg states very clearly that in the fact, or occurrence, of revelation the religions are in agreement; it is in the content, in the nature of what is revealed, that there are deep and radical differences.[21] One would get a very distorted and inadequate idea of the Bible and its revelation from the references in Das's volume. What we know as the gospel, the good tidings which Christianity has commissioned us to make known to men and women every-

---

[19] *Ibid.*, p. 306. Used by permission of The Theosophical Press.
[20] *Ibid.*, pp. 422-80.
[21] *The Authority of the Faith* ("The Madras Series"), I, 115-16.

where, receives no consideration whatsoever. Redemption from sin, the reconciliation of man with God, a reconciliation accomplished by God in Jesus Christ, who revealed the righteousness of God and his hatred of sin and at the same time his love for man the sinner—all this receives no mention, yet this message is the heart of the good news to men who are in deep distress. So long as this remains true and men stand in need of a Saviour who is not provided in the Vedanta, so long must we who are Christians feel pressing upon us the call to proclaim the message of salvation in Christ Jesus.

Chapter Eight

Sense of Mission

Hᴉɴᴅᴜɪѕᴍ has never been listed with Buddhism, Islam, and Christianity as one of the missionary religions of the world. Its sacred books express no sense of obligation to carry its message to people other than Hindus outside of India. The very fact that every Hindu is a "birthright" Hindu would seem to make the attempt to propagate his religion a kind of incongruity. That a few individuals have espoused Hinduism as their own is looked upon as strange and unaccountable. When speaking of the conversion of the well-known and very remarkable Brahmin woman Pandita Ramabai to Christianity, Sarma says, "We are led to conclude that Pandita Ramabai like Mrs. Besant [who was converted to the Hindu way of life] was one of those rare souls who, born in one religion and driven by their past karma into another, feel instinctively at home there." [1]

The Hindu has not provided for the coming of a man of another faith into the fold of Hinduism, and he looks with the utmost disfavor on the conversion of Hindus to other faiths, especially to Christianity. One of the caste rules which strict Hindus look upon as obligatory is that the Hindu should not leave his native land. That many Hindus are doing so in our day is evident in many European countries and on this side of the Atlantic. But in the case of a man who belongs to a strict Hindu family it is not a pleasant anticipation for him to think of his return as he nears his native shores. He faces a very dis-

[1] *Op. cit.*, p. 134.

gusting ordeal—which need not be detailed here—to cleanse himself from the contamination which has been incurred by visiting a strange land and associating with its inhabitants. All this combines to show that any thought of leaving one's country and carrying a message to another does not fit in with the attitude toward other lands and other peoples which is a part of the Hindu tradition.

Hinduism, however strange it may be, is to be found in lands far distant from India. Hindus are living in the Fiji Islands, the West Indies, South Africa, Singapore, Malaya, and elsewhere. They have migrated to these localities either for business or as laborers. In some cases, as in Fiji, the British brought Hindus in to till the soil and reap the crops which the native Fiji islanders seemed unfitted to do. They have grown until they form a community of some 143,000. The story of the Hindu in South Africa is better known. They emigrated to better their economic condition and found themselves unwanted by the Dutch and British and have not had a happy experience. It was there that Mohandas Gandhi first became aroused over the condition of the underprivileged among his people and took up their cause. There he developed his spiritual method of "soul force" (Satyagraha), which later he used so effectively in his campaign for Indian independence. In the Union of South Africa the Indians number about 400,000, most of whom are Hindus. In the West Indies, Singapore, and Malaya their numbers are small; but they have gone for the same economic reasons. In none of these lands has there been any attempt to convert the surrounding population to Hinduism. In fact Hinduism rests more lightly on their shoulders than on those in their native land. We are told and can easily believe that caste rules and restrictions are not so carefully observed as when these Hindus were among their own people, despite the fact

159

that Brahmin priests have accompanied them and seek to meet their religious needs.

It is another story, however, in the little island of Bali, just east of Java and forming a part of the recently organized Indonesian Republic. There Hinduism exists as the recognized religion of the entire island, an island with a population of about one million. It is not known when or how the people became Hindus. Swami Sadananda tells us that "the island of Bali bears witness to the missionary activity of the ancient Hindus." [2] This is very indefinite; all we know is that as far back as can be ascertained, the Balinese have been Hindus and remain such today. Swami Sadananda proceeds to recount the evidences for the presence of Hinduism in Java, Borneo, Cambodia, Champa (Cochin China), Malaya, and Thailand, in most of which Hinduism has disappeared as a living religion, but in which evidences in language, customs, religious rites, and especially in architectural monuments attest the presence of Hinduism centuries ago.

We must, however, be on our guard. There are undoubtedly monuments which are genuinely Hindu, but in most of the countries mentioned there are remains which are Indian but not Hindu at all; they are Buddhist. The two most astonishing architectural monuments are at Boroboedoer in Java and the Angkor Wat in Cambodia. Boroboedoer is purely Buddhist; in the Angkor Wat it is difficult to tell what gods were worshiped. They were probably Hindu, but today the Cambodians are Buddhists, as are their western neighbors in Thailand and Burma. But irrespective of the affiliation of the peoples with Hinduism or Buddhism, Hindu writers are likely to give credit to Hinduism for their conversion on the basis of their conviction

[2] *Hindu Culture in Greater India,* p. 7.

that Buddhism not only is an offshoot of Hinduism but is a part of the religious movement which is essentially Hindu. As Janardan Bhatt puts it in the introductory chapter of *Hindu Culture in Greater India*, speaking of the people of China, who "are adherents of the faith preached by Lord Buddha, which is another form of ancient Arya Hindu Dharma teaching and as such they are Brothers in faith to us, and we can claim them as our Brothers." [3] There is, however, quite a difference between Buddhism, which has been a real missionary religion, and Hinduism, which at no time of which we have authentic records has shown any urge to carry its message to other lands. The Hindu relics to be found in the lands of southeast Asia are more likely the results of the conquests of Hindu kings than of direct missionary propaganda.[4]

With this background we can realize more fully the significance of the notable missionary movement in our day which is being conducted by the Ramakrishna Mission. Without question the cordial reception given to Swami Vivekananda at the World Congress of Religions held in Chicago in 1893 and the striking success of his many appearances before American and British audiences which followed account for the sense of mission. At any rate the Mission is established in the West, a definite attempt to influence men and women to accept the teachings of the Vedanta.

Careful attention must be given to the motives and aims of the movement as stated by the swamis of the order. Swami

[3] P. 3.
[4] See Sir Charles Eliot, *Hinduism and Buddhism*, Vol. III, chapters on the lands mentioned above. Also see Brian Harrison, *South-East Asia*, which brings out very clearly the way in which Hinduism and Buddhism followed or accompanied the Indian merchants who carried on an extensive trade as far east as Java and Bali. Even Indian princes set up their rule in these lands and made Buddhism or Hinduism or a mixture of the two the religion of their little states.

Akhilananda, of Boston, in his volume *Hindu View of Christ* declares that the members of his order in the West come to "share" with those in other lands the religious insights which have been bequeathed to them largely by Sri Ramakrishna. In emphasizing the idea of sharing, the swami calls attention to what he believes is a difference between himself and the Christian missionary who goes to a foreign country "to save men's souls," as he puts it. If he had been better acquainted with missionaries, Swami Akhilananda would have realized that one of the most familiar words used by missionaries to describe their task is just that word "sharing." They too go to a foreign land to share, in their case to share the message of God's love in Christ Jesus with those who have never experienced what this message might do for them. So far as "saving men's souls" is concerned, every missionary knows that he cannot save a man's soul any more than he can save his own. He points to a Saviour who comes with the forgiveness and transforming power which puts a man on his feet and enables him to lead a new life of joy and victory.

The swamis of the Ramakrishna Mission constantly assert that they do not suggest to or ask a Christian to withdraw from the church to which he belongs or to renounce his Christianity. To put it in the words of the official publication *Vedanta in America*:

Vedanta is impersonal, but it accepts all the great prophets, teachers, and sons of God, and all those personal aspects of the Godhead who are worshipped by different religions. It cannot do otherwise, because it believes that all are manifestations of the one Godhead. Accepting all, it does not attempt to make converts. It only seeks to clarify our thought, and thus help us to a truer appreciation of our own religion and its ultimate aim.

Swami Vivekananda in one of his statements was even more specific, saying that his aim was to make better Christians, better Methodists, Presbyterians, and Episcopalians than they were before hearing and accepting the teachings of the Vedanta.

It would be strange if in the long course of its religious history the thinkers of India had not brought to light certain aspects of truth and certain features of man's obligation to God and to his fellow men which would prove of lasting benefit to men in the West. God has not left himself without witness among any people, and this should be particularly true of the profound and versatile and brilliant minds of the leaders of a people as religious as the Hindus. In the midst of the materialism of the age in which we live it is most wholesome to have men asserting the rights and place of the spiritual in the universe and in life. For a people as restless and as nervously at their wit's end as is true of so many among us, the insistence on quietness and peace within, on the lessons to be learned from meditation, with the mind abstracted from the hustle and bustle of the world around us, is of very great value. The flood of books and articles which are pouring from the press in the West along these lines is ample evidence of the need of that phase of the Indian heritage. The presence of the growing number of psychoanalysts and psychotherapists in all our cities is further evidence of the same malady. As Swami Vivekananda often declared, the great lesson which India has to teach the West is spirituality. We can also learn the supreme importance of the soul, the essential being that we are underneath all else, the soul which is the only thing which counts, in contrast with material things which so frequently absorb all or almost all our attention. These attitudes are what the Vedanta stands for, and we may believe that this kind of thinking is a valuable asset in the life of every man.

But when all has been said of appreciation and gratitude for benefits conferred, the Christian cannot stop and shut his mind to other aspects of the Vedanta which make it impossible for him to look with equanimity at the work of the Ramakrishna representatives. These Vedantists strangely misunderstand the Christian position. It is not the question of disapproving or accepting what Christianity teaches but, for example, the unfortunate inability to realize why a Christian should not be "liberal" as the Vedantist and subscribe to the belief that all the religions are essentially the same and that it makes little or no difference whether a man worships Vishnu in Krishna or the Christian God in Jesus Christ. Are not all sincere men worshiping the same divine being after all by whatever names they think of him? For a Christian to take that attitude and act on it would be to wreck his faith. There is something exclusive about Christianity, as already made clear. A Christian believes that in the revelation of God in Christ he possesses an authentic word from the Ultimate Reality, the one God who is the Creator and Sustainer of the universe. He does not deny that sincere prophets of religion in the course of human history and in other religions have been illumined by contact with the same source of all that is noble and good in the world, but what is of the very essence of his faith is that in Christ God revealed himself as in no others; Christ is different from all others. As the apostle Paul put it in speaking of Christ:

He is the image of the invisible God, the first-born of all creation; for in him all things were created, in heaven and on earth, visible and invisible, whether thrones or dominions or principalities or authorities—all things were created through him and for him. He is before all things, and in him all things hold together. He is the head of the body, the church; he is the beginning, the first-born from the dead, that in everything he might be preëminent. For in him all the fullness of God was pleased to dwell, and through him to reconcile to himself all things, whether on earth or in heaven, making peace by the blood of his cross. (Col. 1:15-20 R.S.V.)

This is the Christian's native atmosphere, his vital breath. He is thus conditioned as the result of a long tradition which reaches back through the centuries to the foundation of the Hebrew commonwealth as we find it in the Old Testament. The basis on which the Children of Israel were hammered into one people by Moses and those who followed him was that they had entered into covenant relations with the Lord God Yahweh. This meant on God's side that he would consider the Israelites his chosen people and would stand by them provided that on their part they would worship him and him alone and would obey his commandments. The first two of these commandments are very explicit: "You shall have no other gods before me. You shall not make yourself a graven image, or any likeness of anything that is in heaven above, or that is in the earth beneath, or that is in the water under the earth; you shall not bow down to them or serve them; for I the Lord your God am a jealous God." (Exod. 20:3-4 R.S.V.) "A jealous God"— the comment of A. H. McNeile is significant: "Hosea was the first to teach that Israel was God's Bride. From his time the thought was common. And the divine 'jealousy' is that which makes Him claim an exclusive right over His people." [5] The debatable question as to whether the teaching in the earliest day was a true monotheism (that only one God exists) or henotheism (that only one God may be worshiped by any people, but that there may be other gods for other peoples) need not concern us here. [6] For irrespective of differences of view at

[5] *The Book of Exodus*, p. 116.
[6] The question may be found fully discussed by W. F. Albright, *From the Stone Age to Christianity*, on one side, and T. J. Meek, *Hebrew Origins*, on the other.

this point, all are in complete agreement that for the people of Israel there was only one God and that the first and most debasing sin was to turn to any other object of worship, to go "awhoring after other gods," as the prophets anathematized the practice. There can be no shadow of doubt that after the time of the Second Isaiah the belief of the Hebrew people was a watertight monotheism. Had not that prophet of the Exile penned these unequivocal words:

> I am the Lord, and there is no other,
> besides me there is no God. (Isa. 45:5.)

This is the most important part of the heritage of both Jew and Christian today. As one of the Jewish rabbis put it, this is the one belief for which a Jew should be willing to die.

The temptation to form a kind of syncretistic religion became very strong after the people of Israel had left Egypt and were settled in Palestine and had come into close contact with the Canaanites who were already in the land. These earlier inhabitants were worshipers of various Baals, agricultural deities who were looked upon as the givers of increase in their fields, their flocks, and their families. But unfortunately the worship included sexual immorality, which was considered essential to insure increase in their fields and homes. What these Canaanites said to the Israelites was that as they, the newcomers, ceased to be nomads and became agriculturists, they would have to depend on agricultural deities to make them successful farmers and not on Yahweh, who was a God of the desert and of wandering herdsmen, a God who was also chaste and hated the abomination of sexual irregularity. The idea suggested was not to cease worshiping Yahweh but to add to that worship the cult of the Baal worshipers, a real syncretism.

And then arose Elijah, one of the mightiest figures in the entire history of religion. It was in the dramatic scene at Carmel that the crisis was reached, when the prophet summoned the assembled people to a clear-cut decision: "And Elijah came near to all the people, and said, 'How long will you go limping with two different opinions? If the Lord is God, follow him; but if Baal, then follow him.'" (I Kings 18:21 R.S.V.) And just at that moment one can imagine a modern Vedantist calling out, "Oh, Elijah, hold a minute! Don't be so strenuous and stern. These Gods may have different names, but they are really the same. Men find God in worshiping Baal just as they do in worshiping Yahweh. See how sincere these prophets are. They lacerate their bodies in their earnestness. There is no need to inject discord among people who will live close together in the years to come. Calm down a bit and find a common *modus vivendi* instead of insisting on the exclusive attitude you are proposing." But Elijah saw something else, what the worship of the Baals really meant, a debauching sexual orgy, a debasing of womanhood, the complete loss of the high ethical idealism of the religion of Moses. These two forms of worship could not mix without a degradation of the worship of Yahweh, the righteous God of Israel. A whimsical suggestion was made by the late Francis J. McConnell when Chinese Christians were suffering martyrdom at the time of the Boxer uprising in 1900. He pictured a Christian on his knees ready to receive the death stroke who suddenly looked up and said, "If you wait a moment, I think I can propose a statement on which we can all agree." There comes a time when no compromise is possible; a decision must be made, or else a man surrenders his moral integrity and his loyalty, and these are more important than life itself.

Many times over after the time of Elijah the people of Israel fell away and seemed almost to forget their allegiance to their

God, but never was the tradition lost. Prophet after prophet recalled the people to the covenant between themselves and God, so that since the Exile and down to the present day the Hebrews have resolutely remained true to the one God who to them is God almighty, Creator and Sustainer of the universe, the God of righteousness and lovingkindness to his people. This is the heritage which has come out of the Old Testament and is the foundation on which Christianity is built. There is something exclusive about it which has determined its course through the centuries. Swami Akhilananda seems to be a bit put to it to understand why with such unanimity Christians take this stand, when he declares that "even the most liberal thinkers in the missionary field seem to think Christianity is the last word in religion." [7] How could it be otherwise when men believe that in Christ God has spoken a definitive word once and for all in his Son, our Saviour and Master?

This being the case, is it possible to do away with rivalry among religions? William E. Hocking believes that it can and should be obviated. By a process which he calls "reconception," in which each religion is to think through anew its own meaning, *not alone but together with the other religions with which it comes into contact.*[8] This would be most agreeable to the Vedantist. Bhagavan Das suggests that a small committee representing the great religions should get together and compose their differences and thus start off anew. But looking back over the history of the expansion of Christianity, is it possible to believe that there would be any Christianity in existence today had its representatives been willing for the sake of peace and harmony to compromise its essential message? There are cer-

[7] Op. cit., p. 268. Used by permission of Philosophical Library, Inc.
[8] For fuller discussion see my *The Philosophy of the Christian World Mission*, ch. xiv.

tainly pain and sorrow in the breast of every true missionary to think of disrupting family and community life by presenting a gospel which calls upon men to leave their former faith and confess their allegiance to a God who is so different and who demands a decision so complete that it severs him, it may be for life, from friends and family. But was it not our Lord himself who declared, "Do you think that I have come to bring peace on earth; I have not come to bring peace, but a sword. For I have come to set a man against his father, and a daughter against her mother . . . ; and a man's foes will be those of his own household . . . ; and he who does not take his cross and follow me is not worthy of me." (Matt. 10:34-38 R.S.V.) And was not our Master himself crucified because he took a stand against the leaders of his own people, people with whom he had so much in common?

We face, then, an incompatibility between Christianity and what the Vedantist proposes—the two are essentially different. But it seems necessary to take another step. Undoubtedly these men, sincere as they are, desire to lead us as Christians into a wider outlook, one more suitable to our deepest needs than Christianity is able to provide, so we are told that we need to come to a "truer appreciation of our own religion and its ultimate aim." [9] Here we are again brought to a halt. What is the ultimate aim of Christianity according to Vedanta? It has surely become very clear in the course of the preceding pages that the purpose of the Vedantic mission is to lead those who come for instruction to realize the meaning of and to accept the truth that the Ultimate Reality is Brahman, the attributeless Absolute. We are told that they do not come to our shores to make converts to Vedantic Hinduism; but when an inquirer accepts the

---

[9] See *Vedanta in America* and various other publications.

Vedantic teaching concerning the Ultimate Reality, it is difficult to see the difference between accepting that doctrine and
becoming a convert to Vedantic Hinduism just as a man becomes a convert to Christianity by accepting the God and
Father of our Lord Jesus Christ as the Ultimate Reality. One is
a convert as well as the other; and the result is similar—the one
who accepts the doctrine of Brahman as Ultimate cannot but
give up his former belief that the God revealed in Christ is
Ultimate, and the same is true the other way around. Each viewpoint is essential to the system to which it belongs. A Swiss who
had recently accepted the Vedanta asserted that he still called
himself a Christian but that he believed that the Ultimate
Reality was Brahman and not the personal God of Christianity.
How could he call himself a Christian, which at bottom means
a follower of Christ, when he repudiates the revelation of God
which Christ lived and died to accomplish?

It seems a very innocent thing to say that the Vedantist comes
to us to "clarify our minds" and to help us "realize" the true
meaning of our own religion and its "ultimate aim," but no
more serious challenge to the existence of Christianity in the
world has ever been conceived than just this Vedantic proposal.
What would happen if this teaching should be accepted so that
it became the prevalent belief in the West? It could only be
that the religion of the West would be no longer Christianity
but Hinduism in its modern Vedantic form, "tinctured with a
small amount of Christianity," to use a phrase coined by Emil
Brunner. It is significant to discover how imperfect a conception of the deeper meaning of Christianity is in the mind of
so candid and fair-minded a student as Swami Akhilananda.
When throughout his able volume on *Mental Health and Hindu
Psychology*, Christ is put on the same plane with Krishna, what
is really involved is the complete repudiation of the conception

170

of the person and work of Christ in the New Testament held by all the Christian churches, Greek Orthodox, Roman Catholic, and Protestant. A fuller account of what Christ means to Swami Akhilananda is to be found in his work on the *Hindu View of Christ*. In this high-minded and sympathetic study there are many statements with which the Christian can agree, but there are also those in which the swami fails to understand features which are looked upon by Christians as the very heart of the gospel.

In this volume Christ is classified with Hindu avatars, the Krishna of the *Gita* and Sri Ramakrishna being the examples cited. While the humanity of Jesus is recognized, its presentation is far from what we find in the gospel account. The omniscience of all these avatars is stressed, not taking into account that Jesus never made the claim—he could not have been a real man had he been omniscient. Again, in speaking of these avatars, the statement is made that "there is a little trace of human characteristics in them," which does not do justice to the essential humanity of our Lord. We are also told that "incarnations live an intense life of God-consciousness without any struggle or effort." [10] What of Christ's temptation in the wilderness and his agony in Gethsemane? Other quotations might be given, but these are sufficient to indicate that we have here a very distorted view of Jesus Christ, our divine-human Master. Again, to turn to another aspect of the life of Christ, we are told that "from the Cross we learn that we are to conquer ourselves and not others first." [11] No one would imagine from this account that the cross had any connection with human sin and with repentance and forgiveness or that there was in the experience of Jesus any revelation of the righteous and loving God

[10] Pp. 214, 28.
[11] *Ibid.*, p. 194.

who had sent him to be the Saviour of the world. The chapter on the "Spirit of Easter" deals principally with the problem of overcoming the "limitations in life and the corruptible nature of the body," and this can be done only by our own effort "by changing our consciousness and our relation to the problems of life with the use of mental force." [12] We may also learn from Easter "that a man can overcome and defy death." [13] Christ is presented throughout as in no unique relation to God; there is no resurrection nor any living Christ; he is no higher than Sri Krishna and Sri Ramakrishna.

It is far from pleasant to display these inadequacies. We need, however, to see clearly how easy it is to think of the religions of the world as alike and on the same plane when such interpretations as these bring Christ down from the lofty levels of the New Testament presentation to those of a more or less imaginary figure like Krishna and of a man like Ramakrishna. With all his remarkable gifts, his sincerity, and his simplicity and deep insights Sri Ramakrishna remains on the human level as a teacher and devotee. It does not seem reasonable to state that the mission of the Vedantists in the West is to "clarify our ideas" about our faith and to show us what the "ultimate aim" of Christianity is when our religion is presented with so little insight into its real meaning.

And now in sharp contrast to the historic absence of a sense of mission in Hinduism, the presence of a sense of mission in Christianity is an outstanding and determinative fact in attempting to understand the genius of the religion of Jesus Christ. Jesus restricted his activities to his own land with the exception of a brief visit to the region of Tyre and Sidon, which was a withdrawal from the pressure of his antagonists and not

[12] *Ibid.*, p. 201.
[13] *Ibid.*, p. 217.

to carry his gospel into a foreign country. It has been claimed by Adolf Harnack [14] and others that Jesus did not contemplate a mission to other lands, but this has not been received favorably by many others.[15] Even Harnack would say that there is an "implicit universalism" in Jesus' sayings and that Jesus "shattered Judaism, and brought out the kernel of the religion of Israel. Thereby—i.e., by his preaching of God as the Father, and by his own death—he founded the universal religion." [16] The whole outlook of Jesus was ecumenical. "So there is nothing that is purely local or transient in the ethical teaching of Jesus. It transcends all the limits of space and time. It is adaptable to all nations, to all races, to all types of civilisation, to all conditions. It can never be out of date until man himself is out of date." [17] And speaking of the Fourth Gospel, Harnack says that "it is saturated with statements of a directly universalistic character." [18] One other passage may be quoted: "And I, when I am lifted up from the earth, will draw all men to myself" (John 12:32 R.S.V.). And then there is the Great Commission given in its most extended form at the close of Matthew's Gospel, "And Jesus came and said to them, 'All authority in heaven and on earth has been given to me. Go therefore and make disciples of all nations, baptizing them in the name of the Father and of the Son and of the Holy Spirit, teaching them to observe all that I have commanded you; and lo, I am with you always, to the close of the age.'" (28:18-20 R.S.V.) It is a moot question whether all these are the exact words of Jesus, but there is wide

---

[14] *The Mission and Expansion of Christianity in the First Three Centuries,* Vol. I, ch. iv, "Jesus Christ and the Universal Mission."

[15] For a discussion of the pros and cons see my *The Philosophy of the Christian World Mission,* ch. iii, "Jesus Christ and the World Mission."

[16] *Op. cit.,* I, 43.

[17] L. H. Marshall, *The Challenge of New Testament Ethics,* p. 191.

[18] *Op. cit.,* I, 42.

agreement that Jesus gave expression to these or similar words and that they do correctly summarize what he meant as the founder of a religion which had a universal mission.

The apostle Paul saw more clearly than any other in that day the universal implications of the religion of Christ. He realized that the new faith could not continue, as some of the early disciples in Jerusalem thought it might, closely allied to if not a constituent part of Judaism. He took the bold step of preaching the new gospel directly to Gentiles who had no connection with Judaism. He made the Jewish law inoperative in the life of the churches he founded. In the memorable Jerusalem Conference, as recounted in Acts 15, he carried the church leaders with him and severed the connections with the old law and the religion of which it was an intrinsic part. In one of the accounts Paul himself gives of his conversion on the road to Damascus, he declares that on that occasion the Lord gave him a definite call to the "Gentiles—to whom I send you" (Acts 26:17 R.S.V.), to put it in his own words. This thought of the universality of the gospel message transformed Paul's whole outlook. Every man was to him "one for whom Christ died" (Rom. 14:15 R.S.V.). One of his most magnificent statements is in his letter to the Romans, Christians whom he had never seen: "For I am not ashamed of the gospel: it is the power of God for salvation to every one who has faith, to the Jew first and also to the Greek" (1:16 R.S.V.), that is, all who were not Jews. For was it not true that "God was in Christ, reconciling the world unto himself" (II Cor. 5:19)? Without attempting here to recount the whole trend of the records, a statement in a recent volume will give a summary of what the New Testament stands for: "The key to the understanding of the New Testament documents is that they are the *propagandist literature* of a widespread and successful missionary movement." [19]

There are those who have mistakenly thought that Christianity was constituted a missionary religion by the command of Christ to preach the gospel to every creature. These commands were really more in the nature of the "sealed orders" which in the days before the "wireless" and the radio were placed in the hands of the commander of a warship, to be opened when the ship was well out at sea. They did not constitute the ship a warship; they only gave direction for the immediate mission on which the ship was being sent. What made the ship a warship was the conception and purpose which lay back of its construction. That is, everything in its building and equipment was in accordance with its original purpose. So we may say that Christianity is missionary, not because it received orders to carry its message to all men, but because it was constructed for that purpose. Missions are not an afterthought, but entered into the plan back in the purposes of God far before Christianity or any other religion came into existence. But it was only "when the time had fully come" that "God sent forth his Son" (Gal 4:4 R.S.V.).

What is there in Christianity which makes it essentially missionary? The very fact that God created the world and all the people in it is the fundamental thing. All are God's creatures; they are thereby constituted children of God no matter how far they have strayed away from acknowledging their dependence and responsibility to him. No religion which claims such an origin can be anything but universal in its purpose and scope. It is as universal as creation. What gives the Christian religion its peculiar missionary impulse, however, is its conviction that this one God, the Creator of all men, came into history in the

[19] H. G. G. Herklots, *A Fresh Approach to the New Testament*, p. 15.

person of his Son in an unrepeatable event to do for mankind what could be done only in that way.

This does not mean that God has not and is not coming into human life and making his will known to men irrespective of religious affiliation. His Spirit has always been abroad in the world, and we have ample evidence that chosen men scattered among peoples far and wide have heard God's monitions and have led their followers into truth and a life far above what it might have been had it not been for their visions of higher things. We may even say that every unselfish and noble thought and act everywhere and at all times has been prompted by the holy God through his Spirit brooding over the sons of men. We read that Christ was the "true light that enlightens every man . . . coming into the world" (John 1:9 R.S.V.) and also, "They [those outside of Judaism] show that what the law requires is written on their hearts, while their conscience also bears witness and their conflicting thoughts accuse or perhaps excuse them . . ." (Rom. 2:15 R.S.V.). Conscience in other words may be said to be the voice of God speaking to all men wherever or whenever they are found.

But when all this is acknowledged, and gladly acknowledged, there is far more than this diffused revelation among men. "In many and various ways God spoke of old to our fathers by the prophets; but in these last days he has spoken to us by a Son, whom he appointed the heir of all things, through whom also he created the world. He reflects the glory of God and bears the very stamp of his nature, upholding the universe by his word of power." (Heb. 1:1-3 R.S.V.) Thus speaks the writer of the letter to the Hebrews and in so doing voices the deepest conviction in the Christian heart. Even beyond the revelation of God to be found in the Old Testament prophets, God makes known his nature and will in Christ as the most authentic disclosure of himself that has ever been or can be made. There is the element of finality in this manifestation. We have in Jesus Christ the only perfect incarnation, God coming into the world of men as a human being. It is not a disguise or a temporary appearance but an authentic self-disclosure, so that from the time Jesus Christ appeared, we know what God is like and what his will for men is. Thus did the eternal and unchanging God, the Ultimate Reality, give an unchangeable revelation of himself, so that any attempt to give us more always ends in a fiasco. Our task and the task which has been that of the Church in the past, the present, and to the end of time is that of interpretation and application of what has been conveyed in Christ to the varying and changing needs of men everywhere and at all times.

There can be no watering down of the message the Christian Church is placed in the world to proclaim. A moralism, even though it be sublime in its demands, cannot take the place of the proclamation of the act of God by which he conveyed his love and forgiving grace to humanity. Such a devitalized paraphrase of John 3:16 as the following is to the point: "God so loved the world that he once inspired a certain Jew to inform his contemporaries that there is a great deal to be said for loving one's neighbor." [20] What is the matter with such a statement? It surely fails to take account of the devastating malady in the world, the tragic fact of human wrongdoing, of sin. God's aim in sending his Son into the world was to do something to rescue men from the terrible predicament in which they found themselves through selfishness, greed, heartlessness toward their fellow men, in short through running counter to God's purpose for humanity and sinning against his mercy and his love. Christianity is realistic in facing human nature as it is and in not making light of this basic problem in the life of mankind.

[20] *Ecumenical Studies*, introducing Leaflet No. 2 on *Evangelism*, p. 8.

How different the viewpoint and teaching of the Vedanta philosophy. Sin is not a corruption of human nature which separates man from God and renders him helpless in the face of temptation. The fundamental fact about man according to Vedanta is that he is divine and "has infinite strength and infinite wisdom at his command, if he will use them to uncover his true nature. This nature can be gradually uncovered and known and entered into by means of prayer, meditation and the living of a disciplined life—that is to say, a life which seeks to remove all obstacles to the divine unfoldment." [21] This thought is put in enthusiastic words by Swami Vivekananda: "Ye are the children of God, the sharers of immortal bliss, holy and perfect beings, Ye divinities on earth—sinners! It is a sin to call a man so; it is a standing libel on human nature." He also declares: "The Vedanta says that you are pure and perfect, and that there is a state beyond good and evil, and that is your own nature. It is higher than good. Good is only a lesser differentiation than evil. We have no theory of evil. We call it ignorance." And again, "I am responsible for my fate, I am the bringer of good unto myself, I am the bringer of evil. I am the Pure and Blessed One." [22] Here is one of the weakest spots in all Hindu thinking and practice. Unwilling or unable to face the fact of man's corruption and its dreadful entail in the history of the human race, Hinduism stands powerless in the presence of man's greatest need, the need of an inner transformation which changes his nature and makes it possible for him to live a new life in which he can be and do what was impossible before. The message of the Vedanta is not for the evil man or the weak man, who needs and must have help from the outside. All that can be hoped for is that in another incarnation—it may be a hun-

[21] Vedanta in America, under the second fundamental truth. Used by permission of the Vedanta Society of Southern California.
[22] Teachings of Swami Vivekananda, pp. 165, 224-25, 208.

dred or a thousand lives off—he may be able to rise to the Vedantic viewpoint and start on his way to emancipation.

On the contrary, in Christianity provision is made to meet any man at any time in whatever condition he may be with a salvation which will rescue him from his sinful nature and start him off renewed within and with a new power to live a life of joy and victory. How is this accomplished? God sent his Son primarily to be a Saviour. According to the record an angel announced to Joseph, the husband of Mary, that "she will bear a son, and you shall call his name Jesus, for he will save his people from their sins" (Matt. 1:21 R.S.V.). Man was made in the divine image, but he is not a divine being; he is a creature over against God the Creator. The terrible fact is that he has corrupted himself by the misuse of the power of freedom which came to him as a gift from God. He has become alienated from God, and his primary need is to have this enmity changed into gratitude and love. He is in need, in other words, of reconciliation to God. It is a matter of personal relations, and reconciliation can be accomplished only by the personal God through a Son who can bring man into such a relationship. And here we approach the heart of Christianity, the very core of the gospel message, the unique thing in Christian salvation. How frequently the place of emphasis in our religion is missed; how often the teaching of Jesus is placed in the primary place and the heart of the gospel is passed by. We believe that Jesus was the greatest religious teacher who ever lived, and his precepts must continue to be the standard by which all human conduct is measured, but there is that which goes deeper and lays bare the meaning of Christianity more clearly even than the teachings of Christ.

Christopher E. Storrs, of western Australia, wrote a book with the very suggestive title *Many Creeds, One Cross,* thus laying

179

his finger on the determinative and unique feature in Christianity. It is at the cross that we discover the unique meaning of our faith. It does at least two things; the suffering of God in Christ on the cross gives the clearest insight into the meaning of sin. If the sin of man cost that much agony, it must be an awful thing. A man can see himself as he is in abasement and deep contrition before the cross of Christ. He repents of his sins and may well cry out in the words of Isaiah, "Woe is me! For I am lost; for I am a man of unclean lips, and I dwell in the midst of a people of unclean lips; for my eyes have seen the King, the Lord of hosts!" (6:5 R.S.V.) Again, as he stands convicted of his sin, a man can scarcely fail to realize how much God must have loved him and what possibilities God must see in him to send his Son to die for him. So he is raised up and is filled with gratitude. He begins to learn the meaning of forgiveness; not only is the guilt of his sin removed, but he is made a child of God and taken into the family of the redeemed. He realizes that he is saved not by his own strength and exertion but by a Saviour. It is the experience of salvation which more than anything else gives the Christian the sense of mission. What has happened and continues to happen to him is so wonderful that he feels an inner compulsion to tell to others what may be their experience if they accept God in Christ and are transformed.

In the three Synoptic Gospels, immediately upon the statement that Jesus had "yielded up his spirit," we read in Matthew's Gospel, "And uphold, the curtain of the temple was torn in two, from top to bottom" (27:51 R.S.V.). We need not be concerned with the actual curtain in the Temple in Jerusalem; what the Gospel writer realized was that the curtain between the holy place and the holy of holies was gone. The people up to this time could never see beyond the curtain where the

Shekinah, the "presence" of God, dwelt; but now in the Cross that curtain had been removed, and all men were for the first time able to see God in his righteousness and love as they came to understand the death of Christ. Is there any wonder that Oscar Cullman[23] makes the Cross the central fact of history or that John Bright speaks of it as the "pivot of history"? [24] When to the fact of the Cross there is added the fact of the Resurrection, and we have a living Christ, ever with us in the Holy Spirit, we may enter the more deeply into the meaning of the act of God in Christ Jesus and of the significance of history as the theater of God's saving deed for the salvation of men.

As we approach the end of this brief sketch of the genius of our faith in contrast with that of the Vedanta, it is impossible not to be deeply impressed by a final consideration. The Christian gospel is embodied in a story and is conveyed, when it is most effectively presented, by the telling of that story. The hymn whose opening line is "We've a story to tell to the nations" expresses what is in mind exactly. We are likely not to realize fully the deep significance of this fact about the Christian message. It is unlike the Vedanta, which is primarily a philosophy which must be studied diligently to be understood and accepted and put into practice. Not so with the gospel of Jesus Christ. It is embodied in a story which can be understood by a child and yet which is so profound that the most erudite and wisest scholar will still be gazing in wonder until he passes on to the fruition of his hopes with Christ and the redeemed forever.

And what a story it is! "For God so loved the world that he gave his only Son, that whoever believes in him should not perish but have eternal life." (John 3:16.) Those words speak a language all can understand. And how many thousands and

[23] *Christ and Time*, passim.
[24] *The Kingdom of God*, p. 231.

hundreds of thousands there are today who are singing the praises of Jesus of Nazareth, Son of man and Son of God, who for us and our salvation made the supreme sacrifice and gave up his life that we might be saved from our sins and enter into the hope of eternal life. Through the story we see the ultimate Reality of the universe, the God of righteousness and love, and his Son, our Saviour and our Master, who made him known. As Robert Browning phrased it, "I say, the acknowledgement of God in Jesus Christ accepted by the reason solves for thee all questions in the earth and out of it, and has far advanced thee to be wise." [25] We have a matchless message, for we have an incomparable Christ.

[25] *A Death in the Desert.*

BIBLIOGRAPHY

Akhilananda, Swami. *Hindu Psychology, Its Meaning for the West.* New York: Harper & Bros., 1946.

―――. *Hindu View of Christ.* New York: Philosophical Library, Inc., 1949.

―――. *Mental Health and Hindu Psychology.* New York: Harper & Bros., 1951.

Appasamy, A. J. *The Gospel and India's Heritage.* London: S.P.C.K., 1942.

Archer, William. *India and the Future.* New York: Alfred A. Knopf, Inc., 1918.

Ashby, Philip H. *The Conflict of Religions.* New York: Chas. Scribner's Sons, 1955.

Aurobindo, Sri. *The Life Divine.* 2 vols. New York: E. P. Dutton & Co., 1953.

Authority of the Faith. Vol. I of "The Madras Series." New York: International Missionary Council, 1939.

Ayyar, A. S. P. *A Layman's Bhagavadgita.* 2nd rev. and enl. ed. Madras: Law Journal Press, 1949. Vol. I.

Barnett, Lionel D., tr. *Bhagavad-gita; or, The Lord's Song.* Boston: Beacon Press, 1952.

Besant, Annie, and Das, Bhagavan, trs. *Bhagavad-Gita.* 4th ed. Wheaton, Ill.: Theosophical Press, 1950.

Braden, C. S. *The Scriptures of Mankind.* New York: The Macmillan Co., 1952.

Das, Bhagavan. *The Essential Unity of All Religions.* 2nd ed. Wheaton, Ill.: Theosophical Press, 1947.

Dasgupta, S. N. *A History of Indian Philosophy.* New York: Cambridge University Press, Vol. I, 1922, to Vol. IV, 1949.

Deussen, Paul. *Outline of the Vedanta System of Philosophy.* New York: Grafton Press, 1906.

―――. *The Philosophy of the Upanishads.* Edinburgh: T. & T. Clark, 1908.

Devanandan, P. D. *The Concept of Maya*. London: Lutterworth Press, 1951.

Edwards, J. F. *The Life and Teaching of Tukaram* (with J. Nelson Fraser). Madras: Christian Literature Society, 1922.

————. *The Religious Hunger of India*. Madras: Christian Literature Society, 1948.

Farquhar, J. N. *The Crown of Hinduism*. New York: Oxford University Press, 1915.

————. *Modern Religious Movements in India*. New York: The Macmillan Co., 1915.

————. *An Outline of the Religious Literature of India*. London: Oxford University Press, 1920.

————. *A Primer of Hinduism*. 2nd ed. New York: Oxford University Press, 1912.

Forman, Henry James, and Gammon, Roland. *Truth Is One*. New York: Harper & Bros., 1954.

Garratt, G. T., ed. *The Legacy of India*. London: Oxford University Press, 1937.

Ghanananda, Swami. *Sri Ramakrishna, His Unique Message*. Madras: Sri Ramakrishna Math, 1946.

Hanayama, Shinsho. *The Way of Deliverance*. New York: Chas. Scribner's Sons, 1950.

Harrison, Brian. *South-East Asia, a Short History*. New York: St. Martin's Press, 1954.

Harrison, M. H. *Hindu Monism and Pluralism*. New York: Oxford University Press, 1932.

Hill, W. D. P. *The Bhagavadgita*. New York: Oxford University Press, 1928.

Hiriyanna, M. *The Essentials of Indian Philosophy*. New York: The Macmillan Co., 1949.

Hocking, W. E. *Living Religions and a World Faith*. New York: The Macmillan Co., 1940.

————. *Re-Thinking Missions*. New York: Harper & Bros., 1932.

Hogg, A. G. *The Christian Message to the Hindu*. New York: The Macmillan Co., 1947.

Hunter, A. M. *Interpreting the New Testament*. Philadelphia: Westminster Press, 1952.

Hutton, J. H. *Caste in India*. New York: Oxford University Press, 1951.

Immanuel, R. D. *The Influence of Hinduism on Indian Christians*. Jabalpur, India: Leonard Theological College, 1950.

Indian Philosophical Congress Silver Jubilee Commemoration Volume 1950, also companion Vol. II. To be secured of Prof. N. A. Nikam, Sec'y., Basavanagudi, Bangalore, India.

Isherwood, Christopher, ed. *Vedanta for Modern Man.* New York: Harper & Bros., 1951.

―――. *Vedanta for the Western World.* London: George Allen & Unwin, Ltd., 1948.

Joad, C. E. M. *Counter Attack from the East.* London: George Allen & Unwin Ltd., 1933.

Kennedy, M. T. *The Chaitanya Movement.* New York: Oxford University Press, 1925.

Kraemer, H. *The Christian Message in a Non-Christian World.* New York: Harper & Bros., 1938.

Life. "The World's Great Religions," Pt. I, "Hinduism," February 7, 1955, pp. 58-80.

Macnicol, Nicol. *Indian Theism.* New York: Oxford University Press, 1915.

―――. *Is Christianity Unique?* London: Student Christian Movement Press, 1936.

―――. *The Living Religions of the Indian People.* London: Student Christian Movement Press, 1934.

McKenzie, John. *Two Religions.* Boston: Beacon Press, 1952.

Moore, C. A., ed. *Essays in East-West Philosophy.* Honolulu: University of Hawaii Press, 1951.

―――. *Philosophy—East and West.* Princeton, N. J.: Princeton University Press, 1944.

Nikhilananda, Swami. *Ramakrishna: Prophet of New India.* New York: Harper & Bros., 1948.

―――. *The Upanishads.* New York: Harper & Bros., Vol. I, 1949; Vol. II, 1952.

―――. *Vivekananda: A Biography.* New York: Ramakrishna-Vivekananda Center, 1953.

Otto, Rudolf. *The Idea of the Holy.* New York: Oxford University Press, 1950.

―――. *Mysticism, East and West.* New York: The Macmillan Co., 1932.

Pearson, Nathaniel. *Sri Aurobindo and the Soul Quest of Man.* London: George Allen & Unwin Ltd., 1952.

Phillips, G. E. *The Religions of the World.* Wallington, Surrey, Eng.: Religious Education Press, 1949.

Piet, J. H. *A Logical Presentation of the Saiva Siddhanta Philosophy.* Madras: Christian Literature Society, 1952.

Radhakrishnan, S. *The Bhagavadgita.* New York: Harper & Bros., 1948.

————, and Muirhead, J. H., eds. *Contemporary Indian Philosophy.* New York: The Macmillan Co., 1936.

————. *Eastern Religions and Western Thought.* 2nd ed. New York: Oxford University Press, 1940.

————. *The Hindu View of Life.* New York: The Macmillan Co., 1931.

————. *The Principal Upanishads.* New York: Harper & Bros., 1954.

————. *The Vedanta According to Samkara and Ramanuja* (taken from *Indian Philosophy*). London: George Allen & Unwin Ltd., 1928.

Ramakrishna, Sri, *Teachings of.* Almora, India: Advaita Ashrama, Mayavata, 1948.

Rawson, J. N. *The Katha Upanishad.* New York: Oxford University Press, 1934.

Ross, F. H. *The Meaning of Life in Hinduism and Buddhism.* Boston: Beacon Press, 1953.

Sedananda, Swami. *Hindu Culture in Greater India.* Delhi: All India Arya Dharma Suwa Sariya, 1949.

Sanatana-Dharma, an *Advanced Text-Book of Hindu Religion and Ethics.* No author given, but based on original ed. by Annie Besant. Madras: Theosophical Publishing House, 1940.

Sarma, D. S. *Studies in the Renaissance of Hinduism in the Nineteenth and Twentieth Centuries.* Benares Hindu University, 1944.

Schilpp, P. A., ed. *The Philosophy of Sarvepalli Radhakrishnan.* New York: Tudor Publishing Co., 1952.

Slater, R. H. L. *Paradox and Nirvana.* University of Chicago Press, 1951.

Soper, E. D. *The Philosophy of the Christian World Mission.* New York and Nashville: Abingdon Press, 1943.

Suzuki, D. T. *The Essence of Buddhism.* S. Pasadena, Calif.: P. D. & Ione Perkins, 1947.

————. *An Introduction to Zen Buddhism.* Boston: Marshall Jones Co., 1934.

————. *Living by Zen.* S. Pasadena, Calif.: P. D. & Ione Perkins, 1949.

Three Great Acharyas, Sankara, Ramanuja and Madhwa. Various writers. 2nd ed. Madras: G. A. Natesan & Co., n.d.

Urquhart, W. S. *The Vedanta and Modern Thought.* New York: Oxford University Press, 1928.

Vireswarananda, Swami. *Brahma-Sutras.* Almora, India: Advaita Ashrama, Mayavata, 1949.

BIBLIOGRAPHY

Vivekananda, Swami, Teachings of. Almora, India: Advaita Ashrama, Mayavata, 1948.

Watts, A. W. The Spirit of Zen. New York: E. P. Dutton & Co., Inc., 1936.

———. The Supreme Identity. New York: Pantheon Books, 1950.

INDEX

189